God Talk

God Talk

Extracts from a journal

Peter Francis

BALBOA.
PRESS

A DIVISION OF HAY HOUSE

All scripture quotations, unless indicated otherwise are taken from the HOLY BIBLE NEW INTERNATIONAL VERSION ®. Copyright © 1973, 1978, 1984 Biblica. Used by permission of Zondervan. All rights reserved.

Scripture quotations marked NRSV are taken from the New Revised Standard Version Bible, copyright 1989, Division of Christian Education of the National Council of the Churches of Christ in the United States of America. Used by permission. All rights reserved.

Scripture quotations marked NKJV are taken from the New King James Version. Copyright 1979, 1980, 1982 by Thomas Nelson, inc. Used by permission. All rights reserved.

Balboa Press books may be ordered through booksellers or by contacting:

Balboa Press
A Division of Hay House
1663 Liberty Drive
Bloomington, IN 47403
www.balboapress.com.au
1 (877) 407-4847

Printed in the United States of America.

ISBN: 978-1-4525-1276-1 (sc)
ISBN: 978-1-4525-1277-8 (e)

Balboa Press rev. date: 1/28/2014

Preface

Books are usually written with a specific purpose in mind – biographies, cookery books, 'how to' books etc. In the Christian arena we find books of theology, church history, devotions, missions and prayer – to mention just a few.

This book wasn't so much written as compiled, from prayer journals that I have kept, almost daily, for a number of years. The prayer journal derives out of the time I set aside specifically to sit with God, read His word, and commune with Him in a time of reflection, waiting, listening and conversing. Some days this time is short in duration, maybe less than an hour. Other times it can extend for several hours. This is what I refer to as 'God Time'.

There have been days when this time has given me wonderful revelation of God's love and purpose (often leading me far from the verse of the day) such that I have been blessed beyond measure. This has led me to wonder if others could be touched by my experiences in a beautiful and endearing way.

And so, the book! My prayer is that, as you read and share of my journeying in 'God time', it will encourage and prompt you to not simply join in my experience but to give yourself to Him in a new way, setting aside any agenda you might have in favour of sitting at His feet and allowing Him to draw you further into the intimacy of His love.

May He bless you abundantly.

God... I Am

"Can you fathom the mysteries of God?
Can you probe the limits of the Almighty?
They are higher than the heavens – what can you do?
They are deeper than the depths of the grave – what
can you know?
Their measure is longer than the earth and wider than
the sea."

Job 11.7-9

In these few simple questions and statements is encapsulated the enormity of God. Zophar speaks of the height, depth, length and width of God's knowledge. In Ephesians 3.18, Paul speaks of the height, depth, length and width of Christ's love. In essence, both are limitless.

For me, this passage stands like a rock, a sure reminder of hope, in the sea of Job's hopelessness. True consideration of Job's situation could easily lead to total surrender to the circumstances. And similar scenarios are played out all too regularly in present day living.

Like Job, we need to be reminded of the limitlessness of God's knowledge and of Christ's love. No circumstance removes us from God's knowing. No event can deny us Christ's love.

As far as the east is from the west, so big is our God, and so far-reaching is His love and concern for us.

Lord God,

I come before You in thanksgiving. I thank You for this present reminder of Your might, Your love, and Your presence with us – with me.

Strengthen me in this knowledge. I yearn to see signs, wonders and miracles occur in the name of Jesus. I dare to hope that I might experience, and minister, such happenings.

1

All things are possible with my great and mighty God. I declare Your power and presence – without limit – in all the earth, and in every heart.

Hear the cry of my heart, Lord. Reach out to the lost, and work miracles in their lives, in Jesus' name I ask. Amen.

Daily Life

This is my comfort in my distress, that your promise gives me life.
Psalm 119.50 NRSV

This verse reinforces for me the essential connection between my life in God and my earthly life. When trials befall me and I possibly experience distress, these things are caused by and in this world. Discomfort and disadvantage come out of daily life in the natural. At such times it is not difficult to dissociate God. I may be tempted to think of Him as "high and lifted up", as distant, remote and certainly removed from my struggles. How wrong I would be to think this way. But how eager Satan is to have me think so!

My "life" comes from God's promises. His Word contains the most wonderful encouragement for me. Not least is His constant assurance that He is with me at all times. And this includes, yes especially includes, the rotten and messy situations, the times when I could be tempted (though this is Satan's activity, I'll warrant) to feel that I have so let God down that I can't possibly turn to Him. Anyway, He wouldn't be there for me. What lies!

I have experienced this. I have felt so wretched at one time in particular that I carried for a long time the sense of having let God down. I carried it, that is, until God challenged me with a clear reminder that He had forgiven me, and so should I. How liberating! How wonderful to know something of the extent of His love. And what a reminder of the life that is in His promises.

Loving Father and Source of All Life,

I thank You that You have drawn me to You. I thank You that You accompany me on every step of the journey as I allow You. I thank You for the many and wonderful promises in Your Word that give me life.

Yes, Lord, my life is in You – all of my life. I receive You into my struggles, I look to You in the time of temptation, I rest in You when I am weary, and I seek to abide in You at all times.

Your Word is filled with promises. I seem to discover fresh assurances each day. I thank You for the truth of each and every promise and I pray the reality of all of them into my life.

Thank You, Loving Father, Glorious God. Amen.

Going with God

By faith Abraham, when called to go to a place he would later receive as his inheritance, obeyed and went, even though he did not know where he was going.

Heb. 11.8

Abram believed the LORD, and he credited it to him as righteousness.

Gen. 15.6

Why did Abraham go out? Did he have an idea of God's grand plan for his life? Did he envisage a super-ministry for himself? I think not! In fact, I don't think Abraham's focus was so much on himself. Abraham had faith in God, and his motivation was dependence on God arising from his relationship with God. Abraham "believed" God. I take the literal meaning of this as: to steady oneself by leaning on something. Furthermore, the grammatical form implies continuing permanently in this attitude.

I don't want to be consumed, or even bothered by how I'm going to manage the many worldly concerns and arrangements that crop up. I yearn to follow Oswald Chambers' words:

> "Suppose God is the God you know Him to be when you are nearest to Him, what an impertinence worry is! Let the attitude of the life be a continual 'going out' in dependence upon God and your life will have an ineffable charm about it which is a satisfaction to Jesus."
>
> (Chambers 1927, p.8)

Lord God,

I look to You. I look to relationship with You. I don't want to know what You are going to do. I want to know You – deeply, intimately, personally. I want to trust You completely. I choose to steady myself by leaning on You – permanently. I want to 'go out' continually in dependence upon You. I want nothing to be between myself and You.

Would You help me with this? Please speak to me and guide me. Please show me the way forward. You called Abraham to go to a new place, a strange place. I do not read of him badgering You to tell him where he was going. You told him, and he went.

I believe in You, Lord. I will go out in surrender to You and I will rejoice in the wonderful things You do. I give myself whole heartedly to You. Hallelujah! Amen.

Less than Perfect

Judah the father of Perez and Zerah, whose mother was Tamar,… Salmon the father of Boaz, whose mother was Rahab, Boaz the father of Obed, whose mother was Ruth,… David was the father of Solomon, whose mother had been Uriah's wife…

Matt. 1.3,5,6

The genealogy of Jesus is far from being "pure" in as much as He is directly descended through a pure blood line. I wonder if God used this "varied" descent to illustrate to us how His love can create something pure out of conditions less than ideal.

The thread is continued through Mary's conception while she was betrothed to Joseph. Joseph's initial reaction was to quietly divorce this woman who had become pregnant by "another".

Then the angel of the Lord appeared to Joseph and affirmed the divine origin of Mary's conception, after which Joseph remained faithful to Mary and honoured our Lord with an earthly father and home.

I can be so encouraged by this beginning to the life of the Son of God on earth. My own history is far from perfect, and I continue to make mistakes even as I commit to journey with Jesus. Will God abandon me because of this? I think not! He has said He will never leave me. This is good to hear but I don't read it such that I can be careless in myself. I am in covenant relationship with my maker and I have my part to play out, even though I might do it less than perfectly.

Father God,
As I read the genealogy and earthly origin of my Lord Jesus I take encouragement that my own imperfections do not disqualify me from being healed, cleansed and enjoyed

by You. I commit myself to You in the covenant relationship that we share. I bring my failings before You and I ask Your forgiveness.

The forebears in the genealogy of Jesus were less than perfect, but they were forgiven. How powerful is Your forgiveness!

I look to the journey that is ahead. My desire remains to honour You every day. I ask You to lead me only into those things that You would have me do. I pray that You will continue to mould me into the person You want me to be.

I thank You for times like this present moment when I can quietly sit with You. I may not be fully aware of all that You impart, but may I be ever open to receive.

I thank You for this new day. I surrender it to You, and ask that You lead me. Let us travel together, and enjoy each other. Thank You, dear Father in Jesus' name. Amen.

Hovering

Now the earth was formless and empty, darkness was over the surface of the deep, and the Spirit of God was hovering over the waters.

Gen. 1.2

Since the beginning the Spirit has been there. Before the world began, while still shapeless and devoid of any life, there was yet life – the life of the Spirit of God.

And this is the richest life that is available to man. God has been there for us since the very start. His power was over all the earth. It still is, although it is often hidden and ignored because He has given both Satan and humanity certain power in transient measure.

The power of evil and "the worldly" often threatens. Yet the Holy Spirit remains – mightier than anything else, ready to enter any situation and bring Godly input.

Lord God,

I thank You for Your Holy Spirit and the presence that is so obviously in my life. I surrender in full measure. I ask You to fill me, to overflow me, and to lead me ever in Your Holy Spirit.

Your presence was on the earth before man came into being. I ask You to be active upon the earth today. Your Spirit is needed.

Dear God, please enter into areas of conflict and stress. Please work by the power of Your Spirit to bring relief.

I ask You to be present in the church in fuller measure. Fill the whole of Your Body with Spirit power. I pray for unity and strength. Let the world see the life that is available in You.

You are present on earth, Lord, in the form of Your Holy Spirit. Bring further manifestation. I pray for healings and deliverances, salvations and releases of power. I ask for these things in Jesus' Name. Amen.

Teaching, preaching, healing

Jesus went throughout Galilee teaching in their synagogues, preaching the good news of the kingdom, and healing every disease and sickness among the people.
Matt. 4.23

The threefold ministry of Jesus – teaching, preaching, and healing had begun. Jesus started in His home area of Galilee. He was to go also to Judea and Samaria. He ministered wherever His Father led Him. His sole purpose was to do the will of the Father. He was totally obedient to His calling.

Jesus' teaching was both simple and profound. The gospels are filled with knowledge of God and insight into His ways. Jesus taught often by using parables. The full meaning might escape the crowd, and even the disciples, for Jesus often gave further explanation in private.

His preaching was shared in the ordinary surroundings of everyday life. He would speak from the prow of a fishing vessel moored in shallow waters to the people gathered on the nearby shore. Or He would share God's word with the multitude as they enjoyed a picnic together.

The healing that Jesus wrought seemed the most natural, free-flowing ministry of a loving God. As He says to someone, "Be healed. Your faith has made you whole", we might well respond, "Of course, indeed, our faith is a totally wholesome thing."

What can I gain from this verse and these few recorded observations?

I can learn simple aspects of faith easily from the teachings of Jesus. I need to hold on to these for I believe the foundation of my wonderful relationship with an Almighty God to be a very simple belief in the redemptive grace of God through the sacrifice of Jesus Christ. I can also dig deeper into Jesus' teachings for greater insight, for a further enlightenment and depth of knowledge. The disciples would say to Jesus, "Master, tell us the meaning of this. What did you mean when you said…?"

The ability to ask Jesus Himself for further clarification is not denied me. I can come quietly into my secret place, join with my precious Saviour in worship and adoration and say, "Dear Lord, please show me more! Please take me deeper into Your Word, draw me closer to You, and give me further insight and meaning from Your Holy Scriptures!"

I believe there is as much teaching for me from Jesus as I will seek and receive.

The preaching of Jesus tells me that God's Word is to be lived day by day. Day-in and day-out I can live in His ways. I can seek His will and, as I do so with all my heart and all my soul and all my mind and all my strength, I believe I will find His will. Then it is for me to commit, and allow God's will to meet with my will and be the guiding force in my life.

Jesus brought healing to many who expressed faith for it. There is further revelation in this for me. I realise the gifts of healing and of faith are His to endow, but I will press in and seek further enlightenment from Him.

Lord God,

I come before You in worship and thanksgiving. I thank You for the teaching, preaching and healing of Jesus. I rejoice in the miracle working power of the Son of God, and I worship the Almighty One, the great Creator, the force of the universe, the source of all life, my Heavenly Father and Loving Dad.

I pray that You open my eyes to see clearly all that I can learn of You. I ask You to open my heart to receive, and open my mind to store, remember and recall every good thing.

My prayer is to come closer to You, and to learn more of You. I unashamedly ask for this.

I pray that You walk with me through every day. Make Your Word live in me. Have your way in every aspect of my daily living. Let Your perfect will be done in my life.

I ask these things in the precious name of Your Son, my Saviour, Jesus Christ. Amen.

Taking time

Very early in the morning, while it was still dark, Jesus got up, left the house and went off to a solitary place, where he prayed.

Mark 1.35

This verse holds a significant key to the ministry of Jesus. He took time to talk to His Father. He sought out the Father and His way. And He took His time. In that beautiful pre-dawn period, He found a quiet, secluded place where He was able to join in holy fellowship with the Father. I see how important these times would have been to Him. I understand how vital they are to me, to my relationship with my heavenly Father, and to any work that I hope to do for Him. And this is the order of priority for me.

My relationship with the Father must take precedence over all else. Nothing is as important as this to me. Whether I do anything for Him or not, I press in to deeper relationship and growing intimacy. I want to know Him, to feel His "heartbeat", and to live in unity and harmony with it.

Lord God,

I am not presently in a pre-dawn, solitary place, but I am at peace, and quiet before You. And I know You are here.

I open my heart to You. I seek closer intimacy. I ask You to draw me deeper into the sweetest relationship with You. Is it possible that You might share some of Your divine secrets with me?

I rejoice that my Lord and brother, Jesus, has shown me how to draw aside and to give my whole attention to You. I may not be as able as He is to draw really close to You and to hear Your faintest whisper, but I give myself to the task willingly and joyfully.

Hear my heart cry, precious Father. Know my desire for more closeness with You. Draw me to You. Wrap around me and infuse me with Your holiness. Forgive me my sins and transgressions this day, and lead me forward in Your will and provision. Amen.

Now go

The LORD said to him, "Who gave man his mouth? Who makes him deaf or mute? Who gives him sight or makes him blind? Is it not I, the LORD? Now go; I will help you speak and will teach you what to say."

Exodus 4.11,12

Moses is still complaining of how unsuitable he is for the task that God has called him to. As I write these words, I am suddenly struck by the impertinence that Moses exhibits in challenging God so. – Pray God that I might not do this!

Moses argues that he does not possess eloquence of speech. God counters by reminding him that He gave him all of his senses and He will equip and guide him in what he is to do. What a wonderful, wonderful encouragement this is. I receive these powerful words for myself. I see the revelation in this of God reminding me that everything I have is God given, and God will lead me in all that He would have me do. I take this word very much for me, for today.

Moses, however, was not satisfied. He continued to object (v13ff), and God got angry such that He commissioned Aaron to work with Moses. I would not presume to set myself above Moses, but I do not wish to make God angry. There are likely times that I do, and I confess and repent of these. My deepest desire is to do His will. I pray that I am open, at all times, to hear Him and to obey.

Again I read the words "Now go." God had clearly commissioned Moses, but what of me? I have taken particular note that on two successive days recently the word of the Lord that I have received and meditated upon has said, "Now go." Is this the start of further development in my journey with God? Will I get closer to Him? Will He open up further opportunities for me and lead me into encounters with His Spirit? Will He expand and increase my faith to amazing proportions? Oh, that the answer to all these questions would be, "Yes, of course. Yes, indeed. Yes, yes, YES, and Amen."

Lord God,

I am nothing without You. I love You and I desire to please You in all that I do. Yet I do not always succeed. I know this, and I am sorry. I ask You to forgive me. Forgive me, please, and help me to move forward in You. I thank You for the words spoken to Moses which I receive today for myself. I am reminded that all I am and all that I have come from You. Furthermore, you can do anything whatsoever in me, with me, and through me.

Lord, I feel so willing. Two deep desires in my heart are to draw closer to You, to live in deep and sweet intimacy and harmony with you, and also to bring many others into relationship with You for themselves. I thank You for the opportunities You give me. I am hungry for more. I surrender this to You. I wait upon You. In your time I am ready to receive, and to go. Lead me, glorious Lord and precious Saviour. Let your light shine brightly through me, in Jesus' name I pray. Amen.

Fruit of Repentance

Produce fruit in keeping with repentance.

Matt. 3.8

These words were addressed by John the Baptist to the Pharisees and Sadducees. He called them a 'brood of vipers'. It seems that both groups were unrepentant in their ways, seeing themselves as right, often being critical and patronising. John's message appears like a reminder from God and a prompt for these people to bring themselves into obedience to God.

John the Baptist preceded Jesus. His mission was to prepare the way. Yet I believe his call to repentance has not been superseded by Christ, but rather endorsed and emphasised.

There may be those today who call themselves Christian, yet hold back when it comes to the duty of repentance. I call it a duty for I see it as every believer's obligation to live a repentant life. When sin assails, in any form, our reaction is sometimes to turn from God. This may be out of guilt or shame. I see both of these as the very weapons of the enemy, used effectively to estrange us from God. We need to turn immediately to God, and offer Him our repentance.

God has given me the gift of repentance through Jesus. As I repent He can keep me informed and alert to the way I must go. And I want to go this way. But I cannot do it on my own. I sense God telling me clearly today that I do not have to. It's as if He's saying, ***"My dear child, understand that I have given you the gift of repentance. Added to this, I bring you reminders, through the word of my servants, that I am ever ready to receive your confession and repentance. As surely as the father waited, daily, for his son in the parable of the Prodigal Son, so I wait for you to come to me with repentant heart. Come to me. Let me do what I long to do, which is to release you from your sin. Let me remind you that for this purpose I came to earth. Receive*** *my release, then move on into the fruit of repentance. I have so much for you to do for me. But it cannot happen without your repentance. Come now, I'm waiting."*

Lord, Holy God,

    I hear You call and I know that You are specifically calling me. I repent of all my sins to this moment. I lay them before You in humble confession. I ask Your forgiveness, pardon and release. I would that I could bring before You now all my future sins. I cannot do this, but must continue to repent with each passing day. Lead me, Lord, in a lifestyle of repentance.

    As You forgive and pardon me, may I move forward into the way You desire me to go. I thank You for the many gifts You have blessed me with. Enable me to share this gift of repentance. Let me encourage others to acknowledge and release their sins to You. May the body of Christ be purified. Let us be reminded of the reality of Your cleansing and release, received by us through confession and repentance of sin.

    Come, Holy Spirit, breathe afresh on this earth. Let sinful man be touched again by a sinless Saviour. Set us free. Bring us to full and continuing repentance, in Jesus' name I ask Amen.

Walk with God

Enoch walked with God; then he was no more, because God took him away.

Gen. 5.24

It appears that Enoch did not experience death but was simply "translated" by God from the earthly plain to the heavens. In this, Enoch was most unusual. The only other person not to die was Elijah. Enoch was special to God. He **walked with God.**

This indicates great companionship. For me it compares with Moses being called a friend of God and with David being referred to as a man after God's own heart. These men are among the giants of the Old Testament, and Enoch is with them. Enoch walked with God. He enjoyed God's company and, seemingly, God enjoyed his company.

This is what I want. I want to walk with God, for God to enjoy me and for me to enjoy Him.

Lord God,

I rejoice in meeting with You today. Outside it is stormy and the weather is far from pleasant. Yet indoors, and in my heart, I feel great peace at this moment. I am mindful that, if You are for me, who can be against me?

I ask to walk with You. And my request is not just for an hour or even a day, but for all time. I want to walk with You every day of my life, both here on earth and then in heaven.

I wait on you. I rejoice when You speak to me and I look for You.

I pray that You will enjoy my company and lead me into further enjoyment with You.

Dear Lord, may we walk together today? I ask You to take me and lead me in those ways that will please You. I look for Your will, and only Your will, to be done in my life.

In love, I come in full surrender to You.

Precious Lord, may we go forward together, in Jesus' name I ask. Amen.

Unshakeable Faith

We live by faith, not by sight.

2 Cor. 5.7

This is a simple statement. This is a compelling statement. Faith is a conviction in things that cannot be seen. Faith is believing for the almost impossible. Impossible, that is, without God!

Jesus said, **"With man this is impossible, but with God all things are possible."** (M't. 19.26). I can say, "All things are possible with God." But I want to know, Know, KNOW this. I want to be unshakeable in my faith.

Lord God,

I bring before You my desire for unshakeable faith. I know that all things are possible with You. I want to believe that all manner of seemingly impossible things will happen through You. I pray for a faith to believe for the difference between "can" and "will". I don't want to think, "This can be done in the name of the Lord." I want, O how I want, to think and believe, "This will be done in the name of the Lord."

Lord, I do believe; help me overcome my unbelief.

Great is Your faithfulness Amen.

World, Beware!

The kings of the earth take their stand and the rulers gather together against the LORD and against his Anointed One.

Psalm 2.2

These words were written in the time of the monarchy in Israel, possibly by David, yet they seem so relevant and applicable to modern times.

I feel that the world has lost all sense of moral obligation, loyalty and faithfulness to God. I think many people desperately need a Saviour yet may not admit it, nor even be aware of it.

The precious name of the Saviour, Jesus Christ, is far too often used with disdain, disrespect, and even blasphemy.

Yet the psalmist knew that God would not be mocked, that He rules over all and will ultimately break through.

Ask of me, and I will make the nations your inheritance, the ends of the earth your possession. You will rule them with an iron sceptre; you will dash them to pieces like pottery. (vv.8, 9)

The Anointed One will come again in glory to claim the whole earth. How many will be ready for Him? The warnings are in His word. This very psalm says:

Therefore, you kings, be wise; be warned you rulers of the earth. Serve the Lord with fear and rejoice with trembling. (vv. 10, 11)

The rulers of this world would do well to heed these words. So also would each and every one of us, being careful to **serve the Lord with fear and rejoice with trembling.**

Rejoicing brings joy. Trembling mixes that joy with awe and reverence. What a potent, and right, mix with which to serve our Maker.

Lord God,

You are worthy of the most awe-filled and reverent commitment and service from me. May I serve You in this way, and know joy unbounded as I work in partnership with You.

I pray for the state of the world. I pray for global leaders and ask that You impact them. I pray for monumental revelations of Your truth such that will change their thinking and bring them to a place of understanding, acknowledging and committing to Your ways.

You are the great God, the only God. May the earth take notice. I bow before You, Lord. May I serve You with fear and rejoice with trembling. In Jesus' name I ask. Amen.

The Catch

Simon answered "Master, we've worked hard all night and haven't caught anything. But because you say so, I will let down the nets."

Luke 5.5

A whole night of fishing without a single catch would be a long and frustrating time. Simon and his partners were experts in their craft. They could read the weather and sea conditions and they well knew where to apply the nets in fishing. But this night it was to no avail.

When Jesus made His bright suggestion to Simon, Simon could so easily have responded in ridicule and derision. After all he was the fisherman, not Jesus. But Simon knew better. Certainly, Jesus had not been trained as a fisherman, but I think Simon knew, even at this early stage, that Jesus was something special, maybe even the Christ, the living God among us. It was sometime later when Peter actually declared Jesus to be the Christ of God (Luke 9.20), yet I believe he knew all along that he was walking with someone special. Thus, despite a fruitless night, he could say **"But because you say so, I will let down the nets."** And having done so, the haul of fish was truly amazing. It was so great that it began to sink the two boats that were filled with fish.

And so, this small group of men experience a move, in one night, from a non-result, a total lack of any fruit, to the most abundant catch of fish they had possibly ever experienced. And the one factor that brought this to pass was the Word of God. Nothing changed in the geography of the situation. They were still in the place where they had been all night. What made the single difference between abject failure and the most stupendous success was the word of God. God spoke to Peter and Peter obeyed. Without reference to the circumstances, Peter obeyed. He said, simply, *"But because you say so..."*

What wonder, excitement and joy there is to respond to the Word of God. We give no thought to circumstances and what they might indicate. God's word can surmount and overrule the most negative of circumstances. Like Peter, we must first recognise the voice of God, and then we must willingly obey.

Lord God,

I thank You for this insight today. I rejoice in the catch of fish that Peter and his partners experienced when they were obedient to You.

Lord, I want to hear Your voice. I desire an experience similar to Peter, who walked daily with the Lord. He conversed freely with Him. He was open and even foolish with Him. He was sometimes chided and corrected by Him. Yet, in all, he was deeply loved by Him. Lord, I desire this. I look for this in my daily walk with You.

*But there is more. As I hear Your voice, I want to recognise it as Yours. Please give me this great ability. It is possible to hear You and not know it is You speaking. I do not want this. I want to recognise **each time** You speak to me. Let me clearly hear You, and know that it is You speaking to me.*

And yet more. As I hear Your voice, and recognise it. I want to be obedient to what You say. When You ask me to do something, I want to do it in obedient execution. When You require me not to do anything, I want to know and recognise this, and also be obedient.

I pray that I may daily hear Your voice. Speak to me, Lord. Let me recognise You always, and let me ever be willing to serve You in obedience, faith and love. Loving Lord, hear my prayer. Be with me. Amen.

Provision

If that is how God clothes the grass of the field, which is here today and tomorrow is thrown into the fire, will he not much more clothe you, O you of little faith?
But seek first his kingdom and his righteousness and all these things will be given to you as well.

Matt. 6.30,33

My big, lifelong concern is addressed in this reading. This is my concern with financial provision, my need to **know** that there is ample funding for the entire future. I am aware of the hold of this concern, and also the need to break it. I believe I have seen real progress in recent times, but I know there is more to be done – and today is a further part of the release.

I am challenged by Jesus' call of *"O you of little faith"*. I believe I now have the faith to rely on God's ample provision. I have sort of known this all along, but now I feel ready to experience it, to believe for it.

The second aspect of this reading is to do with my consecration. I do so want to seek God before all else and even today I have seen how other things get in the way. I renew my commitment to seek God's kingdom and His righteousness **before anything else**, and I rejoice for the outcome.

Mighty God and Loving Heavenly Father,

*I thank You for this timely and encouraging reading. I thank You for the ways in which You have been building faith in me. I exercise my faith in belief that You will provide for **all** of my needs and You will do so to the fullest measure. I ask that You would favour me with ever growing faith in this and other areas. I pray that You might make me a true man of faith.*

I seek Your kingdom and Your righteousness, and I ask for Your help that I might grow also in this area. My desire is to press closer to You, to know and experience a deeper, more intimate relationship with You. I ask for Your help. I pray that Your Holy Spirit will guide me and show me my path in Your ways. I want less of the world. I pray that natural yearnings and desires might die down in me, to be replaced by a burning desire for You, Your kingdom and Your righteousness.

Hear my prayer, Mighty God, and help me, in Jesus' name I pray. Amen.

A Peaceful Habitation

My people will abide in a peaceful habitation, in secure dwellings, and in quiet resting places.

Isa. 32.18 NRSV

The prophet has said a lot about judgment and punishment, but he now turns to justice and righteousness. He predicts the outcome as peace, quietness and trust forever (v17).

I have experienced much release and blessing through stilling myself before God, by allowing the quietness to envelop me, giving Him opportunity to cloak me in the peace of Jesus. In this place,

I know He is my strength and my protection. The world and its threats recede as I give myself into His company and keeping. I am safe, and I am strengthened to face whatever may be happening in the life that touches me.

This peace is not always easy to receive. And I may not readily find myself in a place of quietness. If I am not able to quiet the hustle and bustle of a busy life or if the sounds, noises and interruptions of the world will not easily leave me, then I look to bring my inner self to a place of quietness despite the world's turmoil. I focus on Jesus. I look to Him and remind myself of how He brought Himself to a place of quietness in the midst of great distress.

Focusing on Jesus reminds me of His promise to me: ***Peace I leave with you; my peace I give to you*** (J'n 14.27).

He has given His peace to me. When I think about **His** peace, I can conceive of no greater power of comfort and strength. And He's given it to me! But I may not feel it. If this is the case, I then make the deliberate action of appropriating the peace of Jesus for myself. I see the true value of a gift being realised in the receiving of that gift by the beneficiary. Jesus has given the gift. I must receive it.

Lord Jesus,

I thank You for the gift of peace that You have made to me. I receive that gift now. I open myself to be covered by Your peace like a warm and comforting cloak. I know that, as I rest in Your peace, I will receive strength. I will be equipped for the ongoing journey. I will receive the assurance that You are with me and I need not fear.

Help me to relax in quietness in You, to not be afraid of solitude. Let me remember how You joined with the Father so often when You sought Him out in solitary places. It was in these times that You heard His voice and knew His ways for You. Such times are occasions for strengthening and divine reassurance. May I never be fearful of coming aside in quietness and trust to seek You out, to open my heart to You, and to allow You to speak further into my life and guide me on.

Dear Lord, allow me now to experience the fullness of Your peace and all the wonders of God that attend upon Your peace. I ask this in the name of Jesus. Amen.

Religion or Relationship

After the LORD had said these things to Job, he said to Eliphaz the Temanite, "I am angry with you and your two friends, because you have not spoken of me what is right, as my servant Job has."

Job 42.7

NIV Bible Study (1985, pp 779, 780) notes: "Despite Job's mistakes in word and attitude while he suffered, he is now commended and the counselors are rebuked. Why? Because even in his rage, even when he challenged God, he was determined to speak honestly before him. The counselors, on the other hand, mouthed many correct and often beautiful creedal statements, but without living knowledge of the God they claimed to honor. Job spoke to God; they only spoke about God. Even worse, their spiritual arrogance caused them to claim knowledge they did not possess. They presumed to know why Job was suffering."

This note succinctly gives us the significant differences between religion and relationship with God. Religion will cause people to mouth creedal statements – often correct and maybe very beautiful, but of no real worth. Religion is often exercised without living knowledge of God. Religious zealots often claim knowledge that they do not possess.

Relationship with God will give us the truth. It will guide us in all truth for we **know** the truth – Jesus. Relationship gives us living, loving knowledge of God. In relationship with God we can say, as Job did:

> *"I know that you can do all things;*
> *no plan of yours can be thwarted."*
>
> (42.2)

Lord God,

I cry out for relationship with You. My true and earnest desire is to get closer to You, to go deeper with You, to enter into the sweetest, awesome, intimacy with You. And to share this with others.

I pray that You would hear this petition and be willing to bring it to pass. I look to You in love and adoration. I rejoice in You, Wonderful God. Amen.

Salvation

> *"...to open their eyes and turn them from darkness to light, and from the power of Satan to God, that they may receive forgiveness of sins and a place among those who are sanctified by faith in me."*
>
> Acts 26.18

The stages of coming to Jesus are so clearly defined in this verse. Firstly, for eyes to be opened is a pre-requisite. If the eyes are closed, the heart and the mind will likely follow suit. Sadly, many have open sight yet choose not to turn from darkness to light.

They do not surrender the power of Satan for the power of God. Without this step they may not receive the profound personal liberation that comes with forgiveness of sins and, in turn, they are denied a place among the sanctified and the inheritance of such sanctification by faith.

Mighty God,
    I thank You for the simplicity with which this verse presents salvation.
    I pray for those who need to receive from You.
    I pray for all people, but especially those I know. Open their eyes, Lord. Turn them from darkness to light and from the power of Satan to the power of God. Let them receive forgiveness of sins and the inheritance of those who are sanctified by faith in Jesus, in whose name I ask. Amen.

Integrity of Heart

I will walk with integrity of heart within my house; I will not set before my eyes anything that is base.
Psalm 101.2b, 3a NRSV

Psalm 101 is a leader's pledge to God. He promises to be a godly leader, to be compassionate and lead with the qualities that are pleasing to God – love, loyalty, justice and righteousness.

The phrases I have highlighted occur in the first part of the psalm and rightly so, I believe. David starts with himself, and this is where I need to start. In seeing that we take the right approach personally we are fitting ourselves to show by example – surely the most effective witness for Jesus. When I think of sharing the gospel message with people, the words that come to my mind are: "Don't preach to me if you're only telling me. Show me! Show me by the way you live out your life, each moment of it." I may not know who I influence in my Christian journey. I may touch many, or I may not impact any at all. This is not my concern. My desire, and intent, is to live in the way that is pleasing to Him, with integrity of heart, within my own house, and beyond.

Of several dictionary definitions of integrity, I opt for the one that says: The quality or condition of being whole or undivided; completeness.

I seek to be whole in the sense of my wholeness in Him. I want there to be nothing in me at odds with God's way. I'm not in this state of wholeness yet but with His help I aim for it. David talks of integrity of heart. I want my heart to be undivided in God. Walking in God's truth and revering His name with undivided heart is surely walking with integrity of heart.

I commit to doing this "within my house". This is how I conduct myself in the privacy of my own home and in the confines of my own mind. This is how I behave when no one else is looking. I haven't been good at this in the past. Will I fare any better now? I cannot trust myself in this but I know, and stand firmly on the belief, that all things are possible with God.

The journey continues. Yesterday is gone, tomorrow promises like an unopened gift, but today is here now. Today beckons me to travel further with Him, in integrity and love.

Holy God,

I come before You in love and adoration. I thank You for yesterday. I hold tomorrow in wondrous expectation, but I give You today with all my love and attendance.

I echo the psalmist's desire to walk with integrity of heart, both within and without my house. I want to do what is good, honest and true, at all times. I cannot achieve this in my own resources, but I know Your willingness to lead me and Your faithfulness to stay with me. I surrender, Lord. I give myself to Your leading. I ask for Your protection. Know my heart, Lord and lead me away from temptation.

May we travel together? And let us enjoy each other as we go, in Jesus' name I ask. Amen.

Only what is given

To this John replied, "A man can receive only what is given him from heaven."

John 3.27

John the Baptist's disciples were somewhat envious of the success they considered Jesus was enjoying. Though they loved John and greatly admired him, they complained to him, stating that everyone was now going to Jesus who might previously have come to John, and to them.

Whilst John's answer most certainly applies to himself, it also has meaning for everyone. John ably worked with what God had given him and he looked for no more. He knew he was the forerunner. His was not the role of the Messiah.

Jesus received what had been given to Him from heaven and He fulfilled His purpose in every respect. He lived to do the will of the Father.

I have been given salvation by a great and loving God. My gratitude is offered in constant prayer. I believe I have been called for a purpose but I can only live and work with what is given to me from heaven. I believe I can ask, but I am not assured of receiving everything that I ask for. This is God's domain. My task is to take what I am given, to gratefully receive it and to run with it. With John I say: *He must become greater; I must become less*. Praise God!

Lord God,

Thank You for the gift of salvation. I receive it and I rejoice. Thank You for the life You have given me. I haven't always done the right thing and I'm sorry, but You are faithful. You have not left me. Your hand is on me. I thank You.

Thank You for the many gifts You have given me and the opportunities You have opened up for me. My desire is to work for You. I think You know this. I ask for enabling and for opportunities. I long to be active for You. Yet I will receive only what is given to me from heaven. May Your will be done in all of my life, in Jesus' name I pray. Amen.

Rested

And God blessed the seventh day and made it holy, because on it he rested from all the work of creating that he had done.

Gen. 2.3

It was apparently much later (Exodus 16) when the Sabbath became established as an official day of rest. But God introduced the concept very early on. He rested, and He likewise calls us to rest in Him.

There are times to set aside, regularly, and "rest in Him" – to remove ourselves from all else, to put aside invasive and distracting thoughts and to give full focus and attention to Him. I see this as Sabbath rest.

There is also the "resting in the Lord" which will see me through every minute of every day. When I have things to do, I do them as I am resting in Him. This is not easy, but neither is it impossible. And, like many things, it becomes easier with practice. Indeed, the more I am able to "rest in Him", the more I will be able to live out each day fully while "resting in Him"

Dear Lord,

What power and peace there is to be found in resting in You. I come to You for rest. I look for Sabbath rest, for times of focused and dedicated being with You. I pray also for the ability to rest in You as I go about my daily living.

Forgive me, Lord, for I am not yet able to rest in You for every minute of every day. But this does not reduce my resolve in any way. Lead me deeper, Lord. I want to go further in You. Draw me closer. Let me know the joy of resting in You, of living every moment with You.

I am willing. I come to You with a desire to be obedient. Receive me and draw me closer, in Jesus' name I ask. Amen.

Little children

And he said, "I tell you the truth, unless you change and become like little children, you will never enter the kingdom of heaven."

Matt. 18.3

Here, Jesus gives the key to eternity – entry as a little child. What might He mean by this? I think He gives the answer in the following two verses:

"Therefore, whoever humbles himself like this child is the greatest in the kingdom of heaven."

"And whoever welcomes a little child like this in my name welcomes me."

(Matt. 18.4, 5)

The humility of a child is a wondrous thing. It is trusting and unpretentious, naive but not servile.

Jesus says two things clearly here. First, I am to be like a child – humble, trusting and innocent, but without a menial demeanour. Secondly, I am to welcome and embrace others who are like this for, in doing so, I welcome Jesus Himself. This is most telling. This is how Jesus is. The Gospels ring out with the humility and compassion of our wonderful Saviour, but there is a most gracious dignity in all He was and did. And He imbued dignity in others (consider the man of the Gerasenes who was healed of demon-possession, esp. Luke 8.35).

Jesus said, *"Follow me."* I want to follow Him and be as He was.

Lord Jesus,

I thank You endlessly for the supreme sacrifice You made for me. I thank You also for the example You set when You walked on this earth.

I want to follow You, Lord. Please help me to be as the children You talk of in this passage.

*Lead me into true humility without servility. Let me be naive yet wise, trusting You in **all** things, and unpretentious in my ways. Allow me to see, accept and appreciate others who walk like You, and may I witness to You in these things through the power of the Holy Spirit. Amen.*

In the name of...

David said to the Philistine, "You come against me with sword and spear and javelin, but I come against

you in the name of the LORD Almighty, the God of the armies of Israel, whom you have defied."

In all appearances in the natural David seems to be no match for the Philistine in any way. But David realises that the fight is not against purely physical odds. Goliath, as representative of the Philistines, has dared to stand up against Almighty God. David realised this truth early on in the day when he asked the men standing near him,

"What will be done for the man who kills this Philistine and removes this disgrace from Israel? Who is this uncircumcised Philistine that he should defy the armies of the living God?"

(v 29)

David goes into battle against this ugly foe, not in his own strength but in the power of the God of Israel, all-mighty and good and just.

There will be Philistines who will seek to stand in my way and try to exercise control over me. I need to be like David and discern when these threats are not simply against me but indicate blatant defiance of the living God. In such instances the full power and force of heaven is with me, and I may be assured of victory if I will but enter the battle.

Lord God,

I receive this greatly encouraging word from David's story. I receive it, and I thank You for it, for I know it comes from You.

I know also that You are my source. When the Philistine seeks to attack me, I ask for discernment to know that You

have been defied. Let me then go forward into the battle, not
merely reliant upon You, but confident in You that the battle
will be won and the enemy vanquished.

Lord, mighty God, You are my God and my King. I salute
You. I honour You and ask that my whole life might speak
in testimony to Your love, mercy, grace and blessing. Amen.

Knowing

"I am the good shepherd; I know my sheep and my sheep
know me – just as the Father knows me and I know the
Father – and I lay down my life for the sheep."

John10.14, 15

This simple statement says so much. The Father is God. The
Father and the Son are one. There is an exquisite relationship
between them. Jesus is comparing His relationship as shepherd
with us the sheep, as likened to the relationship He has with the
Father. He indicates such a depth of intimacy, in **knowing** the
sheep and the sheep **knowing** Him.

This mutual knowledge – ginōskō (Strong, *1097*) is certainly a
knowledge and understanding of, but it can also indicate approval.
It means to know, to understand – deeply and intimately, and to
approve.

Such is the relationship between the sheep and the shepherd,
between ourselves and our Lord Jesus.

Lord God,
I could so easily be fearful at You knowing me. You would
be acquainted with all my faults and imperfections. This
could lead to chastisement, disapproval and even rejection.

But the shepherd does not treat his sheep in this way. He knows his sheep, certainly in a real way, but in a most loving way. When the sheep strays, the shepherd guides appropriately. When the sheep errs, the shepherd corrects with love.

And so it is between You and me. I know that I act like a silly sheep in so many ways. Forgive me, Lord. And You do! You willingly forgive me and set me on the right track. I thank You for this shepherding. Your love is comforting, but also guiding. You correct me in love. I thank You.

You do more than this. You lay down Your life for me. Thank You, wonderful Saviour.

Please be my shepherd today. Take me, and lead me in the way You have set for me, in Jesus' name I ask. Amen.

Lift your eyes

The LORD said to Abram after Lot had parted from him, "Lift up your eyes from where you are and look north and south, east and west. All the land that you see I will give to you and your offspring forever. I will make your offspring like the dust of the earth, so that if anyone could count the dust, then your offspring could be counted. Go, walk through the length and breadth of the land, for I am giving it to you."

Gen. 13.14-17

Abram has left Egypt with Lot and their families. They are both wealthy, owning many flocks and herds and all the accoutrements of prosperity. Indeed, they had so much in the way of material possession that they found it impossible to live together in the same area.

Abram invited Lot to choose where he wanted to live. Lot made a totally selfish choice. Looking out over the fertile plain of the Jordan, Lot coveted it and chose the whole plain for him and his entourage to occupy.

Abram was left with the seemingly less desirable portion of the land. But Abram had done the godly thing and not acted selfishly. And God looks after those who are obedient to Him. He blessed Abram with all the land he could see.

Furthermore, He promised Abram that his offspring would be numerous, so many that it would be difficult, if not impossible, to count them.

A further revelation that comes to me from this reading is that whatever anyone may choose to do, they cannot stop the outworking of God's plan and purposes. There may be a temporary delay. There may not be. Lot selfishly took what he thought was the best of the land, but Abram received the blessing from God.

Again, there may be a choice here for me to exercise. Do I go the way of Lot, making selfish choices and seeking to fulfil my own destiny? Or do I emulate Abram, seek God in all things, and let Him have his way? I know what I want to do. I need God's help to prevent me from getting in His way.

Holy Father,

Thank You for another revelation and lesson. You have told me not to follow the ways of the world and, truly, I don't want to. I want to follow Jesus. I want to obey You in all that I do.

Daily I pray that You will show me Your ways, and lead me in them. I so want to be with You, to do for You, and to honour You in all that I do. I ask You to prevent anything from getting in the way of my following Jesus, and being who and what You want me to be.

I love You. Please receive my love. Hold me close in your love. Fill me, Let me know You more. Let your love overflow from me and touch all that You bring me in contact with, in Jesus name I ask. Amen.

Overshadowed

The angel answered, "The Holy Spirit will come upon you, and the power of the Most High will overshadow you."

Luke 1.35a

The angel prepares Mary for the action of the Holy Spirit who will influence her. It is descriptive of the act rather than a completed deed. This suggests to me a continuous or ongoing happening, viz. the influencing and ongoing influencing, of the Holy Spirit upon a person.

'come upon': *ĕpĕrchŏmai* (Strong, *1904*) can also mean 'attack'. We may recoil slightly at the thought of being attacked by the Holy Spirit, but I like the positive suggestion in this word. Yes, the Holy Spirit may attack and influence in an on-going capacity. And this 'attack' will lead to an overshadowing by the power of the Most High.

'overshadow': *ĕpiskiazō* (Strong, *1982*) is 'to cast a shade upon, to envelop in a haze of brilliancy, to invest with preternatural (out of the ordinary course of nature, abnormal) influence.

Can I possibly imagine this? The power, the might and majesty, the brilliance of Almighty God enveloping His child in a haze of supernatural influence. This is what Peter and James and John saw on the Mount of Transfiguration – the brilliance of the Mighty One, shining forth in all glory and power.

Lord God,

Dare I ask for an experience such as Mary had? Could I hope for such a happening? I know that something must change in my life. I need (or I feel I need) to release myself more fully to You, to make myself more available. I seek Your help. I cast aside the worldly distractions that seem to fill too much of life. I look to You.

Forgive me, Lord, if I allow other things to get in the way. I'm sorry that material needs seem to involve me so. I look to You for all things. Everything I need will be found in You. I surrender all striving to You and ask You to release me, and lead me in Your way.

I pray for the wonder of Your Holy Spirit to come upon me, that I might be attacked by Your Holy Spirit and filled with, and led by, Godly influence in all that I that I am and do. O that I might be enveloped in a haze of brilliancy of Almighty God, filled with wonder and awe, startled and stunned by Your mighty power and love whilst also filled and anointed to minister for You.

Lord, help me to change those aspects of my life that need to change. I do desire to surrender completely to You. Show me how. Lead me, in Your will and Your way, in Jesus' name I ask. Amen.

Cleansed by the blood

He shall slaughter the lamb for the guilt offering and take some of its blood and put it on the lobe of the right ear of the one to be cleansed, on the thumb of his right hand and on the big toe of his right foot.

Lev. 14.25

The blood of the guilt offering is put on the unclean person in the act of cleansing. Instantly my thoughts connect with the precious, ultimate sacrifice of Jesus in the New Testament.

For you know that it was not with perishable things such as silver or gold that you were redeemed… but with the precious blood of Christ, a lamb without blemish or defect.

1 Peter 1.18,19

I am saved from sin, delivered from condemnation by the blood of Jesus. I am smeared with His blood. His blood stains me and this is the most wonderful realisation. His blood manifests His presence upon me and in me. Dear God, please lead me into further revelation.

Saying that someone's blood is upon you can be seen as a guilt message, but I don't feel this in respect to the blood of Jesus. I simply sense deep thankfulness gushing out from me. I see myself sprinkled, smeared and saturated by His blood all over me. I'm not sure if this is a progression or occasional options. No, I somehow see the sprinkling, smearing and saturating all at once. It is as if all three can apply at any one time. It means life – wonderful, abundant and good life in Him. It may lead to the doing of good, great, even amazing things for Him. Yet the first, and most vital, impact is in being. Through His blood I **am** a new creation. I am cleansed. I am restored in relationship with the Father. Christ, the risen and glorious one, is in me, and I am in Him. I move forward, as He leads me, into the fullness of Him.

Lord Jesus, Holy Saviour,

I rejoice in You. I declare You to be both my Saviour and my Lord. I thank You for the amazing, miraculous gifts of forgiveness, healing and release through Your blood.

I have a sense that I should now be humble, almost pious in thanksgiving. I believe the humility is there yet I cannot assume or adopt a false piety. Rather I feel very, very EXCITED.

*I am bursting under the covering of Your blood. I begin to realise who I am in You whilst, at the same time, I hear You tell me that, as yet, I know very little of who I **really am** in You.*

Sweet Lord, take me and make me Your own. Forgive my sins. Yes, even yesterday I lived in sin. I receive the release that Your blood assures me. I do not accept this lightly. I thank You. I belong to You. Lead me on in You. Oh, may I know increase in You until You fill me completely. Hallelujah! Praise You, Lord. Amen.

Don't just say it...!

"The teachers of the law and the Pharisees sit in Moses' seat. So you must obey them and do everything they tell you. But do not do what they do, for they do not practice what they preach."

Matt.23.2, 3

Teachers of the law and Pharisees were the source of constant harassment to Jesus. They were continually criticising His actions, especially the deeds He performed on the Sabbath. They baited Him with provocative questioning and, in time, they brought about His death. Yet they were the authorised successors of Moses as teachers of the Law. They were ordained as representatives of God to proclaim right ways of living to the people. Jesus knew this and He exhorted the people to obey these teachers and to do all that they said. However, at the same time, He gave them a stern and serious warning. In essence, what He was saying was, "Do what they say, but don't do what they do!" He saw their hypocritical ways. They simply did not practice what they preached. What a sad record this reflection of the appointed men of God of the day makes in the Holy Scriptures. How the genuine believer must have struggled against the hypocrisy of the office. How difficult would it have been to follow the teaching of men who simply did not act in accordance with their words?

And what of today? I'd like to say that all hypocrisy and false witness is gone. But I cannot in truth say so. The believer today must be as diligent and careful as any true believer in any age. Good teaching is vital. Good teaching with good example is truly a Godsend. This must be sought and embraced by us all. Sadly, we do need to be wary of those we follow, checking carefully for the evidence and witness of Jesus in their daily living. Men and women of Godly example are precious and to be respected.

Now, what of me? I can endeavour to follow those things I have just written of. I can seek to live in the very best place with God, always looking to maintain constancy between thought, word and deed. But this is not something I can achieve on my own. I can give it my very best shot, but I need also God's grace. This is the difference I have as a Christian. And this makes all the difference. God Himself has assured me: ***My grace is sufficient for you, for my power is made perfect in weakness*** (2 Cor.12.9). My answer is in Him. My assurance is in Him. I cannot do this on my own, but I know that I can do everything through Him who gives me strength (Phil. 4.13). Do I need His strength? Most certainly!

Lord God,
I thank You for this kind reminder of Your grace. I hear You, even now, telling me that Your grace is sufficient for me. Thank You for this. I offer You my weakness, for I believe Your power is made perfect in weakness. I want to live in the very best way I can for You, presenting a diligent and true witness to the presence of Jesus in the whole of my life.

*I ask for Your help. May Your Holy Spirit attend me as I read Your Holy Scriptures, revealing Your truth to me, and giving me deep insight and understanding. I claim Your very word that Your Holy Spirit will teach me **all** things and will remind me of **everything** You have said to me. I ask also that You would speak intimately to me. I long to hear any special words You have for me.*

I seek Your protection. In myself I am weak and open to be enticed into unhealthy thoughts and deeds. I ask Your protection against this. I pray that Your Holy Spirit will prod me, and alert me when I need to be guarded and cautious.

I want to live right for You, Lord. Hear my desire; help me, in Jesus' name I ask. Amen.

Valleys

You make springs gush forth in the valleys; they flow between the hills, giving drink to every wild animal.
Psalm 104.10, 11a NRSV

The psalm talks of the universal sovereignty of God and His all-encompassing provision. But the words I've noted bring a specific picture to my mind.

I see the valleys of life, those times when, for whatever reason, we feel challenged beyond our capabilities. We are down, and often wonder if we can rise up again. We may even feel like a wild animal – alone, vulnerable, perhaps even hunted or relentlessly pursued. We may sense danger, or realise great need.

This is where, and when, we need to look for the gushing springs, the water of life that brings sustenance and hope. The springs flow freely, and their provision is for everyone.

But I do not see these springs gush forth. I am bankrupt in hope. My valley is dry and there is no sign of water or rain. Where is my provision? Where is my God?

Sometimes I can be so consumed with my immediate problems that I am oblivious to all that has been said or assured to me. I am reminded of God's words that He will never leave me, and I feel a gentle conviction inside that He **will be found** in the darkest, driest valley if I will seek Him and not give up. Indeed, my seeking of him must be relentless. God nudges me by His words through the prophet Jeremiah: *"When you search for me, you will find me; if you seek me with all your heart, I will let you find me."* (Jer. 29.13, 14a).

Valleys are places where I need to exercise resistance against any threat, and perseverance in pursuing God.

Mighty God,

You have said You are there for me at all times. You assure me that I will find You if I am relentless in my pursuit of You.

I pray that I will remember this wisdom when I find myself in the valleys of life. I ask that Your Holy Spirit bring recollection to me. Let me turn to You to receive the strength and the hope I may need.

The springs water the valleys and they do not do it sparingly. They gush forth. There is an abundance. May I know this and experience it as the need arises.

O Holy God, You are there — always. I rejoice in this, and I thank You in the gracious name of Jesus. Amen.

Wholeheartedly

Serve wholeheartedly, as if you were serving the Lord, not men.

Eph. 6.7

In the original letter these words were spoken in respect of human slavery and the attitude to be adopted by the slave in service to the master.

Today, they are speaking clearly, and encouragingly, to me. In terms of the slave imagery of old, I can see myself as the slave of **the** Master, as God's slave. Ideologically, I can see this clearly, but in practice it is often difficult. For the service I am called to by God is often to be rendered to men and women. Generally this is not a problem for me. I love to serve Him and I delight to minister to His people. However, just now and then, thoughts creep in such as being taken for granted, being used etc.

In some years of generally unpaid ministry it has not been difficult to give, and give freely, to God's people. Yet I am aware of the odd occasions when the flesh rises and I feel, ever-so-slightly, used or even abused.

Today I receive God's reminder that I am to serve wholeheartedly – that is with every fibre of my being – AT ALL TIMES. Furthermore, I am to see **all** service as serving Him, irrespective of the human recipients.

Lord God,

*I'm sorry. I repent of those times when I have felt hard done by and taken for granted. I repent and ask Your forgiveness. I ask also for the fullness of Your release of me into the ministry that **You** want me to exercise. I commit to You the whole of my needs. I look to You as my provider and*

I realise Your provision can come in ways that may be quite different from my expectation.

I thank You for the ways in which You have allowed me in the past to work for You and with You. I pray that there might be many, many more opportunities. I ask for these, but only as it pleases You. Receive these sentiments. Lead me on, in Jesus' name I ask. Amen.

The Lord said...!

Then the LORD said to Jacob, "Go back to the land of your fathers and to your relatives, and I will be with you."

Gen. 31.3

As I read this verse my first thought was to wonder if God indeed had spoken to Jacob as clearly and directly as the words indicate. There is no confusion whatsoever in this statement. God speaks to Jacob and He tells him exactly what to do. How could Jacob fail? Isn't this always the way with God? Doesn't He always tell us clearly and precisely what He wants us to do? No!!!

Reflecting upon those times in my own experience when I have struggled to hear God's clear voice (and maybe there have been times when I've been unwilling to acknowledge that God just may not be speaking), I took this verse, at first glance, with a measure of (healthy?) suspicion. Then I read the NIV Study Bible notes (1985, p52), and all doubt was allayed:

31.3 – Every sign Jacob was getting – from his wives (see vv.14-16), from Laban (see v.2), from Laban's sons (see v.1) and now from God himself – told him that it was time to return to Galilee.

Immediately on reading these notes I was reminded of my own experience when God so clearly moved me out of one church, and one denomination, and into another. It took several weeks for God to convince me, but the signs were so clear and God's word was so audible. God was giving me clear direction and, of course, it contained those words which are imperative and absolutely essential – *"and I will be with you."* Hallelujah!

But God does not always speak so clearly and definitely. And herein lies the dilemma and frustration – at least it does for me. I want to hear God declare the most brilliant and amazing plans for my future and ministry. But He seems to be silent. And if God is silent there is surely a reason for it. As I view what is before me in the natural, I have more than enough to get on with. It might be that God is speaking to me, and what He is saying is, *"You have plenty to do for the present. Just get on with it and leave the rest to me."* I don't hear Him say this loudly or too succinctly but, nevertheless, He might be talking. Why don't I ask Him?

What I do hear Him say is *"Come closer."* This I willingly commit to before all else, and with all of my heart. If I am to do anything at all for Him it must be birthed in my healthy, deep and intimate relationship with Him. Before I do anything else I must give myself to Him, spend time with Him, talk with Him and be ever ready to hear His voice and direction.

> *Lord God,*
>
> *I delight to spend this time with You. I hear You call me, "Come closer." Lord, I come. Receive me. Take me into Your arms if You will. Speak to me, commune with me. My deepest desire is to live with You, in You and for You – in the now. May I know You more and more? Please walk with me today, and may we go Your way? I surrender to You. Lead me forward in wonderful partnership with You. Amen.*

Receive the rain

Land that drinks in the rain often falling on it and that produces a crop useful to those for whom it is farmed receives the blessing of God.

Heb. 6.7

There is much for me to ponder in these words. I think of the rain falling on the land that is me, and that might lead me to produce a useful crop. This rain can easily appear to me with an extremely negative impact. At best it can be a nuisance, at worst it takes on the form of the most miserable, soul-destroying experience, that begs the question, "Why me?"

I can be tempted to see the effects of this rain as totally destructive to me and achieving nothing whatsoever for God or for anyone else. And this is where I am in danger of giving in to delusion.

The first words of this verse ***Land that drinks in the rain...*** suggest to me that the land has the option of receiving the rain or rejecting it. In the literal example of land, I see how a hard crust on the earth's surface can cause the rain to run off and drain away rather than sink into the subsoil and impart nutrients and goodness.

Likewise I have the option, when it rains, to raise my protective covering and steel myself against the precipitation. This, of course would deny me receiving any goodness from it. In dire moments even a light shower can appear as the most dangerous storm. This intensifies my self-protective instinct to resist with all my being.

How then can I receive, and drink in the rain, enabling it to produce a crop useful to others? I see the way as that of surrender. I do not resist the rainfall, whether it comes as a brief shower or a sustained downpour. Neither do I surrender to the rain. Rather I yield and surrender myself and the wet weather to God. If I allow it, He will enable me to receive the rain, to drink it in such that goodness can come to me from it. God may then use this good crop to "feed", to encourage, others. As this happens they will be blessed. So also will I be blessed.

Returning to the literal illustration, as the land absorbs the rain, the rain disappears. It's the land that benefits not the rain. As I give myself and my situation to God in trials and tribulations, the antagonistic element will, in time, be dealt with by God. And I will have been further formed by Him, and possibly released from bondages as He works in me. As in my every involvement with God, the choice is mine to make.

Lord God,

I thank You for this revelation of the good crop that can come from stormy weather. I surrender to You in all of my living, on fine days and foul. I particularly seek Your protection and leading when the weather turns bad. In these times give me the courage to come to You and trust You for the right outcome. I pray this in Jesus' name. Amen.

My Choice

"But Lord," Gideon asked, "how can I save Israel? My clan is the weakest in Manasseh and I am the least in my family.
The LORD answered, "I will be with you; and you will strike down all the Midianites together."

Judges 6.15,16

In these two verses the frailty of man is confronted by the truth of God.

Gideon sees himself in actual human terms. The clan to which he belongs is seen as the weakest in the whole tribe of Manasseh. He sees himself as the least important in all his family. This is what he sees. This is who he is.

Then God faces him with a divine truth: *"I, the Lord God Almighty will be with you. Understand what this means. The whole power of heaven will be with you. Every divine resource will back you up. You will face the Midianites and you will strike down every one of them. This is what I call you to see. This is who you are in me."*

I see a choice before me. I can opt for what I see in the natural – what circumstances, society and my own thoughts and actions tell me I am. Or I can receive my sonship in Him, and know that the whole of heaven is with me, that the Lord of all is, truly, my own heavenly Dad. Will I give in to the worldly view? Or, as a true and committed believer, will I receive His Word and know that He is indeed with me?

What do I choose? Surely the choice is obvious. Why would I hesitate?

Lord, Mighty God,

I claim my sonship in You. I welcome and embrace all that You offer me in the glorious relationship You have drawn me into. I thank You with every fibre of my being.

I receive Your presence with me. Wherever I go and whatever I do, may it always be in company with You. Strengthen and equip me in Your love. Journey alongside me please! May Your light shine in me and through me. Hallelujah! Amen.

No lies!

– a faith and knowledge resting on the hope of eternal life, which God, who does not lie, promised before the beginning of time,

Titus 1.2

Paul is talking to Titus about faith and knowledge – the faith of God's elect and the knowledge of the truth that leads to godliness. This faith and knowledge rests on the hope of eternal life which God promised even before time itself.

Paul reminds Titus of this promise, making it quite clear that **God does not lie**.

This is a reminder that, perhaps, I need to refresh from time to time: **God does not lie**.

The Word of God is full of promises which stand for me, and for all who would believe. God has promised and **God does not lie**.

I believe God has given me, both directly and through the words of others, certain undertakings and promises for my own edification and blessing. God has promised thus, and **God does not lie**.

I take hold, I receive anew, everything that God has promised me. I rejoice and I give thanks.

Lord God,
I give You thanks today for this reminder of Your many glorious promises and Your word of faithfulness and truth. You have promised, Lord, and You do not lie.
I thank You. I rejoice. I exalt You and I marvel at who I am in You.
I receive anew every promise that is in Your Word for me. I take again each and every personal promise You have made

to me in every way. I look to go forward in Your promises. I believe in the fulfilment of Your promises to me, each and every one of them.

Lead me, precious Saviour. In power let me minister in You, receiving the outworking of every promise, each in its due time and season.

My love for You overflows.

O Lord, lead me on. Hallelujah! I praise Your Name. Amen.

Injustice

Because their sister Dinah had been defiled, Jacob's sons replied deceitfully as they spoke to Shechem and his father Hamor.

Gen. 34.13

An injustice has been perpetrated on Jacob's family. By violating Dinah, Shechem, even though he seems genuinely to love her, has caused disgrace and defilement on all of Jacob's household. The crime was not perpetrated against just one individual but against a whole clan. Understandably, Dinah's brothers are incensed and seek revenge. Their actions are most ungodly. They approach the Hivites with conniving and deceit. The way to address a wrongdoing is not by deceit.

I don't know what I might have done if I had been one of Dinah's brothers, but I hope I would not have turned to deceitful action. At such a time as this it could be easy to forget or overlook God and to respond, simply and vigorously, out of the flesh. This is the very time to turn God-ward, to seek His face and to ask for His remedy.

It's also interesting to note that Jacob's sons are emulating him. A pattern of deceit is being passed from father to son. This needs to be repented of and broken.

Perhaps these are the two clear revelations for me from this meditation today. Firstly, I ought not to respond to injustice with worldly guile, but rather take the matter to God and seek His way. Secondly, if I am aware of any unhealthy pattern being maintained in me I should confess and repent and ask God to break the pattern.

The sons of Jacob followed through their deceitful thinking by killing every male in the city of Hamor and his people. Their action brought horror to Jacob, causing him to say, *"You have brought trouble on me by making me a stench to the Canaanites and Perizzites, the people living in this land."* (v30)

I would not wish any actions of mine to bring trouble. May God protect me from such.

Lord God,

Again I thank You for Your Word. I rejoice in the ways You speak to me through it.

Before You, I look at my own behaviour especially in times when I have been wronged by others. My prayer is that I might respond appropriately, not resort to deceit or to any of the ways or remedies of the world.

Rather, I want to turn to You, to look to Your face and to seek Your way for me. Lead me in Your way, in Jesus' name I ask. Amen.

Without a Shepherd

*When he saw the crowds, he had compassion on them,
because they were harassed and helpless, like sheep
without a shepherd.*

Matt. 9.36

The illustration of shepherd and sheep would have been very clear
to Matthew's original readers and listeners. They would have been
well acquainted with the image and its meaning.

Even though I live in a more urban and industrial, technological
environment, I can still assimilate the plight of sheep without a
shepherd. The prospect is poignant and pressing. I see, in my
mind's eye, a flock of sheep bleating for the leadership, security
and "mothering" of a shepherd. They are frightened and, in fear,
they panic and risk causing great harm to themselves and to each
other.

It is not difficult to extend the mental picture and embrace
Jesus looking on at this shepherd-less flock of sheep. His felt and
demonstrated compassion manifests, I feel, from a sort of turmoil
deep within Him at their situation. Of course, He's not in turmoil
for He is the Prince of Peace. His heart is at rest for He knows where
they will find the shepherd that is needed so desperately. Perhaps a
better description than "turmoil" would be a stirring up within, a
stirring of the deepest love and concern for the "lost sheep".

As I look around me, I see many who are lost. They don't
all know it and many seem not to be concerned. What can I do
for such as these? I can start with the compassion of Jesus, and
continue in obedience to His command to "Follow me!"

Lord Jesus,
*I ask You to touch me with the compassion You had for
the lost sheep. It might be painful, but I seek to follow You.*

Use me if You will to touch the lost, to minister to the very least of them. Show me Your way and guide me in it. I can do nothing in my own strength and resources. I need Your full enabling. Help me, in Your precious name I ask. Amen.

Sins forgiven

Blessed is he whose transgressions are forgiven, whose sins are covered.
Blessed is the man whose sin the LORD does not count against him and in whose spirit is no deceit.

Psalm 32.1,2

God's wonderful gift of forgiveness is freely given to those who turn to Him in true confession. God will not turn away anyone who genuinely seeks Him out. He waits to forgive, to release and to pour out His love upon us.

The one who comes to God seeking His release and cleansing will be greatly blessed by Him. The one who is open and honest with the Lord has no need of deceit. This is such a liberating way of life. The passage through life will not be free of trial or temptation, but freedom comes from openness with God. As we lay our shortcomings (all of them) before Him we go forward in liberty and blessing. Nothing should hold us back from God.

The psalmist relates how he "wasted away" under the heaviness that was upon him while he denied confession, while he "kept silent". He had no strength. He felt no joy. Fortunately he saw the error of his ways. He repented (v5) and received forgiveness. He is able to rejoice in the Lord. He goes forward in righteousness.

I say again, nothing should hold us back from God. Yet Satan makes it his business to seek to control us. He tells us we are unworthy of forgiveness. He pours shame and guilt upon us. He reminds us of past indiscretions as if to say, "See, your repentance of that didn't do you any good!" Of course, he's wrong. Again and again he's wrong. He knows it, but still he hopes to hoodwink me. I think I'm up to his wiles now.

Even if I were to sin every day for the rest of my life (and I shudder at the prospect), I know that, if I turn to God in confession and repentance, preferably sooner rather than later, then He will forgive me. This is genuine forgiveness, a sovereign act of Almighty God which releases me from the hold of sin into the plan of God for my life. It takes me forward into the fulfilment of my life's purpose in Him. It brings joy and light into my life. It grows me in righteousness. It enables me to freely rejoice and heartily praise and worship my Lord and Saviour.

I can come to God with anything and for anything. I gladly and willingly do so, for I know the joy that is before me as I do this.

I love my Lord, and I thank Him for the wonderful gift of His forgiveness, and the way to receiving that forgiveness that was opened up for me by my precious Lord and Saviour, Jesus Christ.

Praise the Lord. Glory to God – in the heights of heaven and in the depths of my being.

Lord, Mighty God, Loving Father,

I thank You for the immeasurable love You have for me. I rejoice in who I am in You – a child of the King, a prince of heaven.

Yet, like all children, I get dirty and grubby from time to time. Sadly, as much as I'd like not to admit it, I must confess I am no exception. I realise this is no surprise to You. I ponder anew, and seek to grasp more fully, the realisation that my taint and soiling make no difference to the love You have for me. Precious Father, this delights and warms me. It also moves me to want to be a better child to You.

I know I sin. Sadly, I know I will continue to sin, despite my efforts to refrain. But I will not cease in those efforts and I ask for Your help and guidance.

I also lay my sin, all of it, before You in true penitence and ask Your forgiveness. I ask You, by the power of Your Holy Spirit, to convict me each time I sin, and lead me into repentance.

I gladly, humbly receive Your forgiveness. I praise and worship You, O Mighty and Loving God. Amen.

Invitation

"Come, follow me," Jesus said, "and I will make you fishers of men."

Mark 1.17

Jesus invites us to follow Him, but the choice is ours! The invitation is a most definite one and if we respond positively it will require total commitment on our behalf. We cannot half-follow, or partly follow, Jesus. I believe Christian commitment must be total, or not at all.

And what does this mean? I don't believe it necessarily means giving up everything, though this may well be asked of some. To follow Jesus means, essentially, to embrace His commandments, to live as He would or, rather, to live **my** life in a way that is pleasing to Him, and to emulate Him in as much as His entire life on earth was lived in compliance with and fulfilment of the Father's will. This, surely, is a way of life. It need not prevent "normal" living, but it certainly offers a challenging template with which to fashion everyday life.

Obeying Jesus' commands to love God first and above all, with every part of me, and to love my neighbour with the sort of regard I want for myself may not be easy, yet it is not impossible.

Challenges will most certainly arise yet Jesus Himself assures us of His help.

There is something of a promise in this statement of Jesus that, if I follow Him, He will make me a fisher of men. This may happen noticeably, in an acknowledged and recognised public ministry, or it may occur unobtrusively, privately and without fanfare. It matters not which way it comes, just so long as God's will is done. I look to follow Jesus, and be used by Him in whatever manner He should choose.

Lord God,

It is a privilege to be invited to follow Jesus. I accept the invitation wholeheartedly. I ask You to forgive me those times when my thoughts, words and actions do not demonstrate the desire of my heart to follow You. My desire remains to live in the fullness of Your will, to be true to You in all that I do.

I look to walk in Your ways today. Lead and guide me. Let me know Your will if You would. Otherwise, just have Your way with me.

Lead, Lord, and let me follow. In You precious Name I ask. Amen.

A close friend

The LORD would speak to Moses face to face, as a man speaks with his friend.

Exod. 33.11a

These words create a most wonderful picture for me. God is meeting with Moses. He speaks with him and the relationship is like that of a man with his friend. The friendship between men can be powerful, sweet and loving. The friendship between God and man might be all of this, but intensified so much more. No wonder Moses' face was radiant after he had met with God. He radiated the love and the power of God, freely manifest in him through the relationship he enjoyed with the Lord God.

This was not a "once-only" event:

The Lord replied, "My Presence will go with you, and I will give you rest." (v14)

What a wonderful assurance these words would have given Moses. He knew the presence of the Lord. More than this, he knew the intimacy of friendship with the Almighty. And now he is being assured of the continuance of this relationship. God is with him, and will go with him. He will receive rest from God. He will rest in God. I dare to believe that this gracious and most wonderful rest would have been available for him at any time that he was willing to turn fully to his Lord. And what of this rest! It is the exquisite place of complete trust and confidence in our supreme maker. It releases us from all stress and pressure. It relaxes us in His full protection whilst we are being fed with His great and wonderful enabling.

So, what about me? How I long to know and experience God as Moses did; to walk and talk with Him and to know that I am regarded by Almighty God as a man regards a close friend. Yes, this, and even more. I believe I have received a personal assurance that God will be with me. Maybe this entails a sweet and lasting relationship.

Lord God,
I thank You for the relationship that Moses enjoyed with You, and that I can share of this as I read Your Holy Scriptures.

I am mindful of my own walk with You. I receive, with deep gratitude, Your assurance that You will be with me. But I ask for more. I seek a sweet, deep and lasting relationship. I yearn to know You as Moses did, to walk and talk with You in the intimacy of a close friendship. You encourage me through Your Word to ask. And so I ask. I ask that I might know You more, that I may meet with You often and regularly and share the joys of friendship with You. Further, may I be equipped by You to lead others into friendship with You.

I give myself over to Your full and perfect will. Receive me, Lord, as a friend. Use me as a faithful worker, in Jesus' name I ask. Amen.

Behaviour

...if any of them do not believe the word, they may be won over without words by the behaviour of their wives, when they see the purity and reverence of your lives...

Instead, it (your beauty) should be that of your inner self, the unfading beauty of a gentle and quiet spirit, which is of great worth in God's sight.

1 Peter 3.1b-2, 4

Peter is addressing women in respect to their unbelieving husbands. Yet I see an application in His words for all of us.

Jesus has commanded and commissioned us to be His witnesses (Acts 1.8). Some people might respond to our words, but we would be wrong to seek to win people over with oratory skills. What speaks more clearly to all people, Christian and non-Christian, is our behaviour.

Peter calls us to demonstrate by our behaviour that we are true followers of Christ. We show Jesus to the world through the purity and reverence we demonstrate in our lives. It is not an external, cosmetic manifesting such as can be achieved by fine clothes, groomed appearance and the right talk and actions. Rather, it is the outward showing of the inner self. It is the manifestation, outworking, and outliving of a gentle and quiet spirit, and the truth that Jesus is with us.

I need this revelation today and I need the reality of these words to be evidenced in my life. I am no wordy evangelist, nor a bold verbal proclaimer of the gospel. Therefore I hope to witness to all by showing them the person I am by allowing myself a measure of transparency so that what is inside might be seen from the outside.

But, what is inside? How do I know that a gentle and quiet spirit inhabits me? How can I be sure that there is purity and reverence inside which will come forth in my daily living and speak to all people of my witness to Christ? I believe the answers to these questions lie with Jesus Himself.

O Loving Jesus, My Sweet Saviour,

I love You, Lord, and my heart's desire is to be a true, faithful and lasting witness for You. I do not seem to be able to loudly proclaim and evangelise. I ask Your forgiveness if this disappoints You. I do, however, experience great enthusiasm in You and I ask You to bless this and draw out this enabling in me that I might minister to many of the reality of You.

I heed the words of Your servant Peter. I pray that purity and reverence will be fundamental to the person I am and to my life and my living. I pray that You would instil in me a gentle and quiet, but strong, spirit, and I ask You to use me

in ministering to others out of the holiness of the spirit that
You implant in me.

    Lord, I have no clear direction, yet I know that I travel
every day with You. I believe You are leading me to the
realisation of Your plans and purposes for me and, along the
way, the dreams that You give me will be fulfilled.

    I rejoice in knowing You. I ask for opportunities – many,
many opportunities to bring others into a knowledge of You,
and to lead them deeper in relationship with You. I pray that
my own relationship with You will deepen. I open myself to
You for whatever You would do. I say again, I love you.

    Lead me in that love. Please draw me closer to You. In
Jesus' name I ask. Amen.

God With Us

The warden paid no attention to anything under
Joseph's care, because the LORD was with Joseph and
gave him success in whatever he did.

Gen. 39.23

Joseph was in prison. It was not a modern, state-of-the-art facility. It would have been a fearful place. But God was with Joseph and gave him success. Some time before this, Joseph had been sold into slavery by his brothers who despised him. As a slave he had been sold to Potiphar, the captain of Pharaoh's guard. In Potiphar's house the Lord was with Joseph and he prospered, rising to take charge of the household. Potiphar's wife made continual passes at Joseph which he rejected. The spurned woman accused him of assault and this caused him to be stripped of his advantages and be thrown into prison. But we read that God was with him and gave him success in all that he did. We also know that God removed him from the prison and raised him to the highest position in Egypt next to Pharaoh. This reads like a Hollywood script, but it is far, far more reliable than Hollywood's make-believe.

God's Word tells us that all things are possible with God (M't. 19.26). We know that God works for the good in all things for those who love him and are called according to his purposes (Rom.8.28). God worked His purposes in Joseph's life in the face of, and despite, amazingly difficult physical circumstances.

I determine to "lift my eyes" to the living God and to look, not on my physical situation, but to Him, knowing that He can do all things.

Father God,

I receive this reminder at this time when the whole year is before me. I go forward into this year believing for all good things to unfold as I move forward in Your purposes for my life.

I thank You for Joseph. I pray that I might know some of his wonderful resilience, faithfulness and trust.

I trust You, Lord. I thank You, and praise Your name. Amen.

Compassion

Jesus had compassion on them and touched their eyes. Immediately they received their sight and followed him.
Matt. 20.34

Compassion is the Greek word splagchnizŏmai (Strong, *4697*), which literally means to have the bowels yearn. This is not only the most graphic vocabulary; it is also quite extreme in what it conveys to me. This "compassion" is more than a simple association in sympathy with someone, or even a demonstration of great pity for a person. This is gut-wrenching, heart-stopping, bowel-yearning for someone in their need and infirmity.

Jesus "had compassion" for many. Indeed, I would suggest He had compassion for all those He saw – He has compassion now for all He sees.

And His compassion is not empty. Another quality He has in as strong a measure as compassion is power. In His power He simply – yes, quite simply – reached out and touched their eyes. The blind men instantly received their sight and, upon doing so, followed Him.

I believe anyone who sees Jesus clearly has no option but to follow Him.

Oh, that the blind might see, and the deaf hear the good news of the Gospel of Jesus Christ!

Father God,

I come to You in thanksgiving and rejoicing. I thank You that You have drawn me to You and brought me into a real, and loving, relationship with Jesus. I thank You for His many qualities but, today, I especially thank You for His compassion, and for the power He has to reach out, in the simplest of actions, and give sight to the blind. I thank You that He does even more than this. I thank You that Jesus restores sinful humanity to right relationship with You.

I thank You for the many who have come into this relationship. I further cry out for others. I ask You to enable and empower me to show them the love, compassion, release and healing power of Jesus. I pray for all those who don't know You. I ask that You draw them to You and use me, if You will, to be a human face of love to them. Amen.

Fast and Pray

"Go, gather together all the Jews who are in Susa, and fast for me. Do not eat or drink for three days, night or day."

Esther 4.16a

The Jews have been threatened with extermination by Haman. Mordecai has passed a message to Esther that she must act. Esther's response is, in effect, "fast and pray" with me.

Whenever any action is required, our first response should be to fast and pray, to touch God and to seek Him in whatever course we should take.

Lord God,

I confess that fasting and praying is not an automatic response with me. Praying comes readily but fasting seems more difficult.

I ask Your help with this. Would You move on me and lead me into fasting. Let it be real for me, and enable me to incorporate it into my lifestyle. I ask this, earnestly seeking it, in Jesus' name. Amen.

Following Him

But the man who looks intently into the perfect law that gives freedom, and continues to do this, not forgetting what he has heard, but doing it – he will be blessed in what he does.

James 1.25

The Christian lives under God's moral and ethical teaching. This is based on the Old Testament moral law, essentially as embodied in the Ten Commandments, but brought to completion (i.e. perfection) by Jesus Christ.

The way of life for the Christian is quite simple. Jesus said, "Follow me." This is all we need to do. It is a simple thing, but not an easy thing to do.

Jesus lived a sinless life. James defines sin for us: ***Anyone, then, who knows the good he ought to do and doesn't do it, sins*** (Jas. 4.17).

This, for me, is the clearest definition of sin. It is so simple, but again, not easy to comply with. Jesus lived a simple life. His purpose during the whole of His life here on earth was simply to do the will of the Father. He has set us an example, and in the verse I have selected for today, I believe James is showing us the way to follow Jesus' example.

God's law is perfect. Jesus did not come to do away with the law. He lived by the law in every respect. But He did more. He lived by grace. Paul reminds us it is by grace we have been saved. Grace operates in the life of the Christian, every Christian. Let's consider God's law under the gift of grace He has given us.

James tells us to "look intently" into God's perfect law. The word in the Greek is *parakyptō* which literally means "to stoop sideways". The stooping suggests to me an intent, and an intensity. There is commitment in this word. It is not a casual look; it is a look with determination to follow through, to enact, and to comply.

James also tells us that the perfect law gives freedom. God's perfect law ensures freedom from sin. We may not achieve God's perfect law in our own strength. But we are further empowered by God's grace, which frees us from sin. It is by God's grace that we are saved. Jesus, the sinless one, gave Himself for us, thereby paying the price for sin.

God's grace allows us freedom from sin. It can lead us as we stoop to look intently into His perfect law. God's grace will uphold us and strengthen us to continue to look into His law and to want to keep this full and perfect law.

James tells us not to forget what we have heard, but to do it.

As we look to God's law and as we move forward with a real intention to live a Godly life, obeying His commands and seeking to fulfil His ordinances, I believe He will cover us with His grace. He will assist us. He will look down from heaven and guide and protect us. He will make His face to shine upon us. He will release divine grace into our lives. He will look on us and give us the sweet peace of Jesus. He will bless what we do.

Lord God,

I thank You for the grace You have extended to me. I thank You for the grace that kept me safe when I chose to walk apart from You. I thank You for the grace that brought me back to You, and the grace that, even now, leads me in the process of sanctification.

I pray that Your grace will strengthen me as I look intently into Your law. I ask for wisdom that I might understand Your law in its application to life today, and particularly to my life. I ask that Your Holy Spirit lead me into all truth and empower me and enable me to live by the truth.

My desire is to live a simple, Christian life. This seems so difficult for me to do on my own. I acknowledge, however, that I am not on my own. Your Word says You will never leave me nor forsake me. Your Word challenges if You are for me, who can be against me?

I claim Your Word, precious Lord. I remind You of the promises You have made to me and I ask You to lead me forward in Godly, Christian living. Amen.

Eyewitness

We did not follow cleverly invented stories when we told you about the power and coming of our Lord Jesus Christ, but we were eyewitnesses of his majesty.

2 Peter 1.16

Peter lived and experienced Jesus and the wonder of His being, together with the supernatural events that marked His life. Peter was an eyewitness to the love and power, the grace and majesty of God, worked on earth among us by His Son, the very image and manifestation of God.

Peter did not have to make up stories in order to spread the incredible news of Jesus' gospel of salvation. He did not need to fabricate events nor manufacture situations. He had no call on myths or imaginative stories. He simply spoke from his first hand experience of Jesus. His Lord and Saviour had been also his companion and friend. Peter had countless eyewitness accounts that he could share of the influence and impact of Jesus in, and on, his life. Peter had only to speak the truth.

This is speaking to me. Is this, perhaps, because my name is also Peter, or is this mere coincidence? However, this Peter can learn from that earlier Peter. He spoke of what he had seen and witnessed of Jesus. I too have experienced Jesus. He has shown me much and done many great and wonderful things in my life. I have "seen" Him, but perhaps not in the physical and tangible way that the apostle Peter experienced. Yet, I truly believe, He is every bit as real for me as He was for Simon Peter.

I may not truthfully describe myself as an eyewitness for Jesus, but I can most certainly be an "I-witness" for Him.

What must I do? I think I simply follow the example of my famous namesake and speak what I know. Like him, I do not need to make up stories. I have many stories of my own real experience of Jesus. My witness comes forth as I share what He has done for me.

Precious Lord, Loving Saviour,

You are real to me. O, I praise You! I thank You for the wonderful gift of salvation You have given me. I thank You for the many, glorious experiences I have shared with You. I thank You for the releases and healings You have brought into my life. I am free. You have liberated me.

I pray that You will enable me to share my experiences of You. I pray for specific, God-appointed and anointed opportunities to share the love of God and the wonderful gift of redemption and salvation that is instantly available through Jesus.

Allow me to share You as I know You. I pray for wisdom, that I do not share inappropriately. I ask also for grace, that my stories will impact, and be used by You to draw people to Jesus.

Thank You for Your incredible love for me. I love You. Amen.

Utmost fear… and love

The fear of the LORD is the beginning of wisdom; all who follow his precepts have good understanding. To him belongs eternal praise.

Psalm 111.10

For me, fear of the Lord is a deep and holy reverence. It is a profound respect for who He is and the power He wields. Yet it is more, for from His position of supreme power and authority, He showers love and grace, mercy and blessing upon me. This truly takes my breath away. This brings me to a place of utmost fear.

I am not always deserving of His love. Indeed, I wonder if the times when I truly deserve His love are any at all. I am quite good at deluding myself to my own behaviour. But, praise God, He can see through all of my delusions. And yet He loves me.

Lord God,

I know I have a fear – a holy respect – for You. Yet, as in many things, I ask for more. I claim Your promise that I will receive if I ask in the name of Jesus. I believe it is right to fear You. I believe that this is proper and I also believe it is right to have faith that all Your promises are true for me. They are "Yes" and "Amen". I ask therefore for more fear of You and more faith in Your promises, and more expectation of their outworking.

Lord, I believe, but I earnestly ask You to help me in my unbelief. Remove all barriers and obstructions. I am ready to go forward with You. I seek the fullness of Christ in me and the power that He promised me in the Holy Spirit.

O God, you are so good. You are wonderful beyond measure. Draw me close. Feed me, nourish me. Let me know the fullness of Your provision in me, for me and through me.

I rejoice in You as the mighty God. Hallelujah! Fill me to overflowing with Your presence. Hear my passionate plea, in Jesus' name. Amen.

Like the wind

"The wind blows wherever it pleases. You hear its sound, but you cannot tell where it comes from or where it is going. So it is with everyone born of the Spirit."

John 3.8

What a practical physical illustration this is for a spiritual truth. Wind is free. It is uncontainable and unpredictable. Wind can go where it pleases. Its sound can sometimes be heard but its source, direction and intent can never be fully understood. There is a power with the wind that defies full understanding. It cannot be controlled or limited.

Jesus tells us that everyone born of the Spirit will be like the wind. In particular He declares that no one will tell where we come from or where we are going to. Only God knows this. Only God can determine how He will use us as we submit ourselves to the power of His Holy Spirit. With God all things are possible. In God we are free and uncontainable. His plans for us can be most unpredictable. **He** is God, we are not. He may direct or lead us just where He will.

There is a power that we can receive from God following our birth in the Spirit. It is His power not ours. The power of God has one specific purpose – to enable witness to Jesus Christ, to spread the Gospel of Good News and to bring the lost to Him. The power of God is a power to save. It is a power to heal, to repair, to mend and to restore. It is a power to strengthen and release. It is a power that can impart all manner of giftings and abilities.

People everywhere are searching. Many have no idea what they are searching for. This is part of the reality of being lost. But the lost do not need to remain lost. Those who know God have been "found". Those who have found new life in the Spirit are equipped, God equipped, to reach out to the lost with the good news. This is not an act of human will and enabling. This work is ordained and empowered by God, through His Holy Spirit.

I am willing; I am eager and expectant of being filled with the Spirit and led by Him to touch others in many places with the life and the love of Jesus.

Lord God,

I invite You to fill me to overflowing with the presence and power of Your Holy Spirit. Like the wind, I would delight to go anywhere, everywhere under Your control. I surrender control to You, This is scary, but I do it. Just like the wind, I do not know where I am heading. I cannot direct the power force in my life. I look to Your Holy Spirit power and I believe for miracles of healing and salvation. May I be a faithful witness to my Lord and Saviour, in whose name I ask this. Amen.

Indwelling

"But will God really dwell on earth with men? The heavens, even the highest heavens, cannot contain you. How much less the temple I have built!"

2 Chron. 6.18

All mighty, all powerful God fills the heavens to bursting point. And we seek to hold Him on earth!

Solomon refers to the magnificent temple he has built, and I think of the temple of the Holy Spirit that is within me. I ask the same question as Solomon, "Will God really dwell with me?"

I know the answer to this question. My God – this God for whom even the highest heavens are too small – finds a place in my heart. He is in me. He will stay in me. He has assured me, "I will never leave you not forsake you." And I can abide (rest, remain, be nourished) in Him.

Solomon, when he had completed the temple, dedicated it to the LORD God and invited God to come to His resting place. His prayer was answered most powerfully: ***When Solomon finished praying, fire came down from heaven and consumed the burnt offering and the sacrifices, and the glory of the LORD filled the temple. The priests could not enter the temple of the LORD because the glory of the LORD filled it.*** (2 Chron. 67.1, 2). Wow! And, "Yes, please!"

Lord God,

I thank You both for Your transcendence and You immanence.

I thank You that You are Lord of the universe, and Lord of my heart.

I dare to hope that Your glory would fill this temple that is my body. Come, Lord, dwell in me. Thank You. Amen.

Not in Vain

As God's fellow workers we urge you not to receive God's grace in vain.

2 Cor. 6.1

This verse causes me to reflect how I might receive God's grace in vain.

I may do this by living for myself. I may do this by not fully taking hold of the redemption that Christ has given me, by not allowing the good seed to take root and to flourish in my life.

When I came to Jesus I made a choice and a decision. I may receive God's grace in vain if at any time I choose to reverse that decision.

I see all of these as valid reasons for receiving God's grace in vain, yet the reason that most impacts me is that I might receive His grace in vain by not manifesting Christ fully in me, by not allowing my practice to fulfil my profession as a Christian. If I speak it with my mouth but do not live it by my life, nor show it by my actions, then I have received the grace of God in vain. God forbid that I would ever do this.

Lord God,

I acknowledge the grace You endowed upon me when You brought me to salvation through Jesus, my Lord and Saviour.

I want never to feel that I have received Your grace in vain. I ask You to lead me in all truth. I bind my will to the will of God. I bind my mind to the mind of Christ. I confess Christ in me and that is sufficient. I believe my growth in Christ comes as I submit myself completely to the Christ that is in me. I do not believe that there is more Christ to enter me, but more release to me of the Christ already there.

If this thinking is wrong, I ask You to change it. My prayer is to become more Christ-like, to release the full power and presence of Christ in my life, to live for Him, to live in Him, to live through Him.

Lord God, show me the way. Enable me to receive and release the full measure of Christ in my life, in Jesus' name I ask. Amen.

Occupation

So Joshua said to the Israelites: "How long will you wait before you begin to take possession of the land that the LORD, the God of your fathers, has given you?
Joshua 18.3

Joshua seems to be impatient with the apparent inactivity of the Israelites in getting on with what God has for them. Through conquest, God had given them the land, but they needed to follow through in possessing it. Seven of the Israelite tribes were still to receive their inheritance.

The whole assembly of the Israelites gathered at Shiloh where Joshua spoke to them, and urged them to further action. Conquest of itself was not enough.

The NIV Study Bible (1985, p.315) notes that conquest had to be followed by settlement.

Settlement involved a survey, a fair distribution, and then a full occupation of the land.

I see parallels with whatever the Lord God may give individuals today. I believe the first step is to know and understand exactly what it is that the Lord is giving. Then settlement needs to occur. We survey the gift, taking in the full scope of it. We make distribution – maybe of time and resources. Then we move into full occupation.

Lord God,

I pray that I might take full possession of all that You've given me. Help me to see the magnitude and scope of the gifts that You have bestowed on me. Help me to experience full measure in You, in Jesus' name I ask. Amen.

Confident

But the Lord is faithful; he will strengthen you and guard you from the evil one. And we have confidence in the Lord concerning you, that you are doing and will go on doing the things that we command.

2 Thess. 3.3,4 NRSV

In this letter Paul has already pointed out to the Thessalonians some of their shortcomings. He will further this before the letter ends. He also gives then directions for overcoming. He tells them clearly here that he expects them to obey his instructions.

But also, as Paul does regularly in his writings, he turns away from our difficulties to the God upon whom we must all depend. In using the very name of the Lord, he reminds us of the One who deserves, and indeed demands, that position of authority and guardianship in our lives. Yes, the Lord is my guardian. He will look after me. I can feel safe for He protects me, He directs and guides me, He is the way for me.

Paul reminds the Thessalonians, and us, that our great and gracious Lord is faithful. For me this means, firstly, that He is always there, and He will always be there. But His faithfulness is not restricted to His presence with me. In His Word He has set out many promises to me. His faithfulness is such that He will, in time, fulfil each and every promise.

He will strengthen me. He will guard me from the evil one. This is so encouraging. So often when I tussle with the contrary thoughts in my mind, the leanings of the sinful nature that seek to draw me into Satan's power, I feel as if the fight is my personal challenge. Of course, I am not up to it, and so I struggle. I need to realise, and walk in the knowledge that God is with me. He knows all the grubby details of my thoughts and

He will help me. He will fight with me. Indeed, He is ready to do this at any time.

I think it might be this knowledge of God's intimate involvement in all of our life, the clean and the not-so-clean that prompts Paul to state his confidence **in the Lord** that we will do the right thing.

I cannot ignore or minimise the difficulties that confront me and will continue to confront me. But I can lay hold of the character of my Lord God and know that He is greater than my lack of will power or my total integrity. He is greater than any of the wiles of the devil.

On Paul's encouraging, I choose to place my confidence **in the Lord** and not in my own feeble nature and insufficient ability.

There are several prayers that Paul breaks into at different stages of this letter to the Thessalonians that I feel to record. In the midst of his identifying of difficulties with the Thessalonians, and his issuing of directions to them, Paul spontaneously opens in prayer for them. There is an immediate focus to this prayer, a focus that I adopt for myself today.

> *Now may our Lord Jesus Christ himself and God our Father, who loved us and through grace gave us eternal comfort and good hope, comfort your hearts and strengthen them in every good work and word.*
>
> (2 Thess. 2.16, 17)

> *May the Lord direct your hearts to the love of God and to the steadfastness of Christ.*
>
> (2 Thess. 3.5)

> *Now may the Lord of peace himself give you peace at all times in all ways. The Lord be with all of you.*
>
> (2 Thess. 3.16)

The grace of our Lord Jesus Christ be with all of you.
(2 Thess. 3.18)

Lord God,

I salute You and honour You as I come before You in this time of prayer. I offer myself fully to Your Lordship. I ask You to be Lord of all of me: Lord of my mind and all of my thoughts; Lord of my emotions and all of my feelings and reactions; Lord of my will and all of my behaviour; Lord of my spirit and my relationship with you.

I look to Your many promises to me, and I claim each and every one.

I ask You to strengthen me. I know You do, and you will continue to. Guard me, Lord, from the evil one and empower me to fight, with You, against his wiles, his deceits, and his dishonesty.

The truth is: I am a child of God. I am Your son. My Dear Father, I bow before You in grateful thanks. Amen.

God's Way

So Gideon took the men down to the water.
Judges 7.5a

I find this to be a most remarkable statement in the story of Gideon. Gideon saw himself as least in his family which was part of the weakest clan in Manasseh. Yet God had commissioned him as a mighty warrior. God's purpose for Gideon was that he should annihilate the forces of Midian.

Before Gideon's troops are amassed we read that *the Spirit of the LORD came upon* him.

Thirty two thousand men had assembled under Gideon. This in itself is quite a statement of support for the least son of a weak family! God did not want the battle waged with such a high number of combatants else the Israelites might think they had won by their own power. God sought to reduce the Israelite numbers. In the first purge, twenty two thousand troops went home, leaving ten thousand with Gideon. This was a dramatic reduction. I wonder what effect it had on Gideon's confidence. He could well have said, "Phew, that's quite a reduction. Let's leave it at that!"

God was not satisfied. The remaining ten thousand men were far too many for God. This is when He said to Gideon, ***"Take them down to the water, and I will sift them for you there."*** I could well understand Gideon remonstrating rather loudly at this point, perhaps saying, "Lord, that's enough. I've already lost the greater proportion on my men." Does he do this? No, in total obedience he "took the men down to the water."

I see this brief phrase as the most amazing statement of faith. Gideon – the least of the weakest – is transformed into God's warrior.

It's not how I see me that matters. It's how God sees me, and how I respond to Him. I can remonstrate with Him in disbelief or I can, in faith, offer myself completely to Him and be led by Him, in total obedience, in all that I do.

Lord God,
I am Yours. I give myself fully to You. Whatever Your plans and purposes are for me, I will in faith follow You. I rejoice in You. Hallelujah! Amen.

Drawn!

He said to him, "If they do not listen to Moses and the Prophets, they will not be convinced even if someone rises from the dead."

Luke 16.31

A rich man has died and is suffering in hell, whilst a beggar who previously sat at his gate has also died but is now in heaven with Abraham.

The rich man calls to Abraham for help. Firstly, for the beggar to come to hell to refresh him. When this is denied he asks for specific messages to be sent to his father's house to warn his five brothers. In responding as above, Abraham is effectively saying that if a person's mind is closed and Scripture is rejected, no evidence – not even a resurrection – will change them.

And so it is today. Many people have not heard the gospel. But many, especially in the Western world, have some familiarity with the stories of God and of Jesus. Many people know that the Bible contains the basis of the Christian faith, and many have heard of the resurrection of Christ. Yet they remain cold. I believe it is God's revelation that will draw the lost to Him. Jesus tells us clearly, *"No one can come to me unless the Father who sent me draws him."* (John 6.44)

Certainly awareness of the Scriptures and the true witness (sensitive and considerate) of Christians can inform a person but only the Father can draw them to Himself.

There are so many that need to be drawn. Many, I know, know nothing of the story of Jesus. Some have scant background knowledge, whilst others have had real experience in the body of Christ, the church, and maybe have even been hurt or put off by such experience. I believe all of these need the drawing of the Father – to Himself and into the body of His Son.

Lord God, Holy Father,

I pray for those who do not walk with You. I cry out for them. I cry out for them. I want to see them in right relationship with You. Would You touch them?

Would You break into their lives and draw them to You? I earnestly pray for their salvation. I humbly ask that You would touch them soon, impact them with the power and wonder of Your love, and draw them to You.

O Great God, hear my prayer. My plea is that none shall perish. In Your bountiful mercy, forgive this sick world for turning from You, and draw them back to You. May all of heaven focus on the salvation of all the earth. Touch people everywhere. Draw them to You. Take them into sweet communion and the deep intimacy of belonging, in Jesus' name I ask. Amen.

Everyday God

But we prayed to our God and posted a guard each day and night to meet this threat.

Neh. 4.9

From Nehemiah I am seeing the power of living and walking with God.

At the start of his book, when he hears of the trouble and disgrace that has come upon Jerusalem, he turns to God in anguish and prayer. When he is moved to do something about Jerusalem he is led by his prayer. When the king asks what his request is, he seeks God before he answers. He answers the taunts of his enemies with confidence in God. When he fears that the work might be threatened by enemy action, again he turns to God in prayer, while he also takes positive practical action by posting a guard day and night. When he learns that the nobles and officials were disadvantaging the people he challenges them to walk in the fear of God.

In Nehemiah I see trust in God demonstrated in a clear and encouraging way. I see him walking with God in every aspect of life. This is my aim and desire. I'm not there yet, but I am encouraged by Nehemiah. Because he looked to God, because he trusted God he was not without problem or difficulty. Yet he was confident in his God. And he didn't leave it all to his God. He also applied himself to practical action that helped his situation. I am encouraged by Nehemiah.

Lord God,

I thank You for the example of Nehemiah. I see how he moved always in dialogue with You. I note how he implemented practical action when it was necessary. I pray that I might achieve the right balance between what I must do and what I leave for You to do, committing everything to You in prayer. I ask You to help me in this.

I thank You as I sense the Scriptures showing me more. I sense a greater insight. I am aware of growing revelation. I pray for more. I ask You, Almighty God, to open my mind to the Scriptures, and to bring Your revelation through them.

I thank You, in Jesus' name. Amen.

God has made clean

The voice said to him again, a second time, "What God has made clean, you must not call profane".

Acts 10.15 NRSV

Peter has received a vision from God. It is obvious that God desires Peter's attention and wishes to show him something of great significance.

What Peter sees is a large sheet coming down from heaven and containing **all kinds** of four-footed creatures, reptiles and birds. Peter is encouraged to eat from what is offered, but he recoils. He remonstrates that he has never eaten anything that is profane or unclean. It is then that God reminds him that He has made things clean.

The trance illustration seems to be about food but it is clear that God extends his cleansing power to mankind as well. When Peter addresses the Roman centurion Cornelius and his friends and relatives he tells them, "…God has shown me that I should not call **anyone** profane or unclean."

As I read of the vision Peter received in his trance, I see, in my mind's eye, an enormous sheet being lowered from heaven containing all manner of human life – all races, all social classes, law-abiding and otherwise, privileged and abused, healthy and not so healthy, and all denominations – and I hear a voice from heaven saying, *"These are my beloved. Go into all the world and love them as I have commanded you."*

Peter's vision resulted in the first salvations among the Gentiles. What, I wonder, will my vision lead to? I don't think I need to know. I simply need to be obedient, to be willing to go where He sends me, and to do His full and perfect will. O yes! Hallelujah!

Lord God,

I am mindful that You have made me clean. Your love has cleansed me. Your love continues to purify me, for I surely continue to get myself dirty.

I look to You for vision. And I look to You for the outworking of any vision You would give me. I want to serve You and I want to do so with all of my being. But, like Peter, I am likely to recoil. In my weakness, then, I offer myself. Take me, show me and lead me, in Jesus' name I ask. Amen.

Assurance

Then Gideon said to God, "Do not be angry with me.
Let me make just one more request. Allow me one more
test with the fleece. This time make the fleece dry and
the ground covered with dew."

Judges 6.39

Gideon asks for another sign. He has already placed the fleece, asking God to cover the fleece with dew and to keep the ground dry. This is precisely what happened. God answered Gideon's request and assured him that he was truly hearing from God.

Now Gideon's asking for another sign. What's with this man? He's certainly showing us that he's far from the mighty warrior that the angel of the Lord called him. One gets the early impression that Gideon is something of a wimp. He certainly doesn't show up differently with his ongoing doubts and fears. These verses tell us much about Gideon.

But, as I reflect on them, they also tell me a great deal about God. Some may be tempted to see Gideon's actions here as testing God. I do not see this. What I do see is a weak and insecure man being commissioned by God for a mighty task, and being so afraid that he seeks God's affirmation – twice!

I also see the patience and love of God as He complies with Gideon's requests, and brings to him the assurances he so desperately seeks. God knew Gideon so well. He knew the man's reactions to His request could well have placed him in a state of anxiety, even panic. He knew Gideon would need full and positive assurances that God was indeed calling him to something that he felt was way beyond him, and which truly frightened him. God knew Gideon, and He patiently and lovingly worked with him to give him the assurances he needed.

I then look beyond Gideon and I see myself, standing slightly to the side and wondering what it might be that God will require of me. Having reflected on Gideon's experience, I can rest in the knowledge that God also knows me, even better than I know myself. He knows me and He knows what I might need in the way of assurance or affirmation. The same love, grace, mercy and patience that God has shown to Gideon, and countless others, is there for me. His attitude toward me is tender, caring and loving. If I need assurance from God I can ask for it, many times over if necessary. For God knows me, and He loves me too much to deny me the responses I need from Him. He led Gideon on to great things. I wonder what He'll do with me!

O most loving God,
*   I thank You for this revelation of love. Gideon was so unsure that he asked You – twice. I am allowed to be unsure, and I can ask You for assurance, confirmation or direction as many times as needed until I am sure that I have clearly heard You. I thank You for this. I love You. Amen.*

Built on rock

"I will show you what he is like who comes to me and hears my words and puts them into practice. He is like a man building a house, who dug down deep and laid the foundation on rock. When a flood came, the torrent struck that house but could not shake it, because it was well built."
Luke 6.47,48

The person who builds their life on the words of Jesus – hearing them, receiving them, and putting them into practice – builds a firm and sure foundation which will withstand all attacks. Many things might attack and seek to undermine and bring down, but the "house" will not be shaken for it is founded on rock, and it is truly well built.

Those who follow Jesus may not have an easy life, but they will live solid in love and in truth; they will live a life of integrity, knowing peace in themselves and peace with others.

The Word of God is a sure footing, a light for the way and an encouragement at all times.

Dear Lord,

Your Word is a lamp to my feet and a light for my path. I thank You.

I seek to build my life on this foundation that is You. I seek Your guidance. Let me dig down deep into You and know You intimately.

May I hear all that You would say to me. Give me, please, a willingness to accept Your words to me, and to be open to anything that You would have me think, say or do. Give me the courage to follow through, and the peace that comes only when I am obedient to the Father's will.

I pray for all those who would follow You. May they give themselves to You in unqualified measure. May they ever be led by You. I thank You and praise Your Name. Amen.

Out of Egypt

And God said, "I will be with you. And this will be the sign to you that it is I who have sent you: When you have brought the people out of Egypt, you will worship God on this mountain."

Exod. 3.12

God is commissioning Moses for a mighty task. He appoints him to lead the Israelites out of Egypt. They were initially drawn to

Egypt through their need for food and the promise and assurance of being fed in Egypt. But Egypt was an alien place and in time the Israelites became enslaved to the Egyptians who mistreated and abused them.

God had a special place for His people, a good and spacious place, a land flowing with milk and honey. It was God's wish for Moses to lead the Israelites out of Egypt so that they might occupy the special place God had for them. God assures Moses. He gives him a sign of His anointing: when Moses has brought the people out of Egypt they will together worship on the mountain where God is presently speaking to Moses. And the most powerful support and encouragement God has already given to Moses. He has said, "I will be with you."

God does not want me to dwell in the wrong place any more than He did the Israelites of old. He has a right place for me to reside and to live in the plans He has for me. I have a choice in this. I can go His way, or I can follow my own path. I choose His way. I have done it my way and it doesn't satisfy. I want to live in His land of promise, and not in any alien place. As I commit to this I just know that He will be with me.

Heavenly Father,

You led Your people out of an alien place, through many long years in the desert, and into the land of milk and honey. And You will do so for me. I choose Your way. Whatever it may involve, I give myself to go with You. Lead me through. Strengthen and support me through desert experiences, and bring me to that holy place where I will worship You in praise and thanksgiving.

I thank You, in Jesus' name. Amen.

The Living Word

For the word of God is living and active. Sharper than any double-edged sword, it penetrates even to dividing soul and spirit, joints and marrow; it judges the thoughts and attitudes of the heart

Heb. 4.12

God's wonderful word is contained in the Bible. It is fully available to me. As I read it, and as I allow the Holy Spirit to guide me into all truth (John 16.13), God reveals Himself to me. God's Word is living and active.

The Scriptures are essentially the written word of God, but there is also available to me the spoken word. Jesus became flesh; the word became life and dwelt among us. Jesus is the word of God. I would have delighted to have walked and talked with Jesus during His short time on this earth. But, as I ponder those times, the remote chance of being in the same geographic area as Jesus and, perhaps, the even more remote prospect of being close to Him, I realise that I might well have missed out.

This is not so today. I have accepted Jesus as my Saviour; I have confessed Him as my Lord. I was blessed by a loving Father with the most wonderful revelation that gave me absolute assurance that Jesus is real. And so, this real, living Word speaks to me today.

Indeed, the Word of God is living and active. God speaks to me through His written word, by specific revelation in particular times – times when He knows I need clear guidance or assurance from Him, times when He reminds me of His love and concern for me.

God speaks to me through Jesus. Sometimes by a particular revelation from the words of Jesus contained in the Bible, sometimes through words I believe Jesus Himself conveys to me, into my mind or into my conscience.

God speaks to me through His Holy Spirit. This is God's manifest presence on earth with us today. The Holy Spirit can move directly in me, stirring my spirit to receive instruction and direction from God. The Holy Spirit can speak to me through other people, through events and circumstances. I believe God, through His Holy Spirit, opens doors for me, He strengthens me, He enables me. But it all comes back to His Word, and my hearing of His Word.

God's word may be encouraging, but it may also be convicting and rebuking. God's word is sharp. When God encourages through His word, it is a "sharp" encouragement. It penetrates deeply through uncertainty and indecision. When we receive God's word of encouragement we **know** that we have heard. The peace of Jesus enfolds us in a gentle but sure confidence. We are released to move on in God's plan, ready to obey His word. When God convicts us by His word, possibly rebuking us also, it is done in love, and justly. We **know** that we need correction. And, if our hearts are right, we will receive and follow through in whatever correction He prescribes. Often such a time is followed by God's word of affirmation and encouragement. God's word is just. As He filters and sorts the thoughts of my mind and the attitudes of my heart, I should freely co-operate with Him. My desire is to know Him intimately, to walk with Him, to converse with Him, to work in partnership with Him, sharing Him with all who are open. I know I am not worthy, in my own standing, to receive and enjoy this sort of relationship. But I receive His word. I have accepted Jesus, the Word incarnate, and He enables me to go forward in right, loving, growing relationship with the Father. As I do this, I crave more of the written word. I give myself over to it. I open myself up to the working of God's Holy Spirit, that He might lead me in thought and deed, through circumstances, events and other people. I look for Jesus. I look (and expect) to hear Him in my inmost thoughts, in my conscience. I look to meet Him in other people, to be strengthened by Him, to be led forward into the fulfilment of my life in Him.

I surrender to God. I heed His word, in whatever form it comes to me. When I need to repent and submit to His correction, I pray that I will do so graciously and willingly. I pray that I am ever open and attentive to receive His word of edification and instruction. I love those times when God speaks to me afresh from His word. I may have read a passage many times yet, on a particular reading, He might bring me such revelation and clarification, insight and direction that I am excited beyond belief. Yes, God's word is indeed living and active – Yes! Yes! Yes!!

Praise God for His true and living Word. May He speak to me today, and to all who would be open and willing to hear from Him. May He continue to speak to us as the days unfold. May we be willing to hear and to respond. Let us be diligent, willing to receive correction and follow through, thirsty for instruction, ready for direction.

May God's Holy Spirit be ever active, constantly guiding us into the truth, into all truth, into the very presence of Jesus, and into ongoing, fruitful relationship with the Lord God.

Almighty God, Loving Father,

I thank You and praise You for Your word, the many forms of Your word. I thank You for the written word, Your Holy Scriptures. Lord, I thank You for the many times and the different ways in which You speak to me from Your word.

Thank You for the word made flesh in My Lord Jesus. Thank You that You have made Him real to me, and He continues to be so real. Speak to me, Jesus. I love You. I am devoted to You.

Thank You, Lord, for Your Holy Spirit, Your manifest, magnificent presence here on earth with us today.

Thank You, Lord, that I hear 'Your Word'. You speak to me through events and circumstances, other people, writings and happenings.

Your love and care for me is so very, very obvious through the different ways in which You speak to me.

I pray that I may always be open to hearing from You. I pray that You will continue to share Your Word with me, loving me, extending me, growing me.

*Help me, Lord, **always** to hear You, in Jesus' name I ask. Amen.*

Find rest

Find rest, O my soul, in God alone;
my hope comes from him.
He alone is my rock and my salvation;
he is my fortress, I will not be shaken.
My salvation and my honour depend on God;
he is my mighty rock, my refuge.
Trust in him at all times, O people;
pour out your hearts to him,
for God is our refuge.

Psalm 62.5-8

Psalm 62 has long been one of my favourite psalms. I have chosen to reflect on the central passage where the psalmist speaks forth an exhortation to himself and then to the people.

The psalm begins with a declaration along similar lines to what the psalmist now exhorts. It is as if he is saying, "This is the truth. Now I exhort myself to receive and live in this truth. God is all I need. He is my very foundation and my life and this is how I must accept him."

The words "find rest" are suggestive of silence, silence in repose. I can rest silently and quietly in God's full keeping. It reminds me of Paul's rejoinder that I am to be anxious for nothing. Silent rest implies a deep and effective repose. There is no stress, strain, or striving. This psalm is one of the great expressions of simple trust in God. I'm pleased that God spoke to me through these words a long time ago. He spoke to me then, and He speaks to me now.

The significance of the psalmist exhorting himself before others is also applicable for me. I must know that I trust God before I can ever encourage others to do so. And that trust applies at all times, in any situation, whatever the visible circumstances suggest or yield. My God is greater than any diverse, threatening or simply unhelpful situation that I might find myself in. In God, alone, will I trust. He is surely and truly my refuge and my strength.

Lord God,

I am mindful that Your mercies are new every morning. I thank You for this as I come to You in renewed statement of my trust in You. I sense a move from reason and sight to faith and trust in the unseen. You are unseen, yet I know You are there. I rejoice in the relationship I have with you. I ask You also that our relationship might become even deeper. Hear my request to go further with You. My humble desire is to get so close to You that I might hear and feel Your heartbeat. And of course I wish to live fully in time with that beat. Your love amazes me. I receive Your love. I thank You deeply and sincerely for Your concern and care of me. I thank You for grace that receives me in Christ even though I am unacceptable in myself. In Christ I am alive, I am clean and I am able to go forward with You. Let me live for You — today and every day. Receive my further statement of trust in You. Increase that trust and faith in me, in Jesus' Name I ask. Amen.

Grow Strong

No distrust made him waver concerning the promise of God, but he grew strong in his faith as he gave glory to God, being fully convinced that God was able to do what he had promised.

Rom. 4.20,21 NRSV

Paul is talking about Abraham. What a wonderful example Abraham is! In Paul's words Abraham's body was as good as dead and Sarah was barren in the womb. Yet, Abraham knew that God had promised him issue, and that was good enough for him.

I connect particularly with Paul's words that **No distrust made him waver concerning the promise of God**. This suggests that there might have been distrust, indeed even a series or number of distrusts. Notwithstanding what might have arisen, we are told that nothing caused any wavering on the part of Abraham. He was sure. He knew what God had promised him. He grew strong in his faith. He stood firm. He was fully convinced. There was no distrust, no doubting that God was able to do what He had promised. Abraham gave glory to God.

There are many aspects of Abraham that I should like for myself.

Lord God,

I thank You for the wonderful example of Abraham. I pray that I might emulate his good characteristics. I feel I can do this as I take further hold, and understanding, of the God I can trust. I want to know You, Lord. You are faithful. You are trustworthy. You have plans for me. You make many good promises to me. All of this I reach out to. I embrace You. Draw me closer, Lord. My faith and my trust are growing. I pray for even greater increase. I pray, in Jesus' name, for more growth in You. Amen.

Supernatural power

No one could see anyone else or leave his place for three days. Yet all the Israelites had light in the places where they lived.

Exodus 10.23

The plague of darkness is the ninth of the plagues that God brought upon the Egyptians in the time of arranging the departure (exodus) of the Israelites from Egypt.

We might assume that Pharaoh was particularly ignorant or pig-headed, yet the truth – of which we are constantly reminded in the Scriptures – is that God had hardened his heart. Consequently, however willing Pharaoh might have been in his own person, his feelings and reactions were over-ridden by God moving supernaturally in his life. The supernatural power of God moved also, in each one of the plagues, to protect His chosen people from calamity.

In this present instance total darkness covered the land of Egypt for three days (a most significant time!). The Egyptians could see absolutely nothing for the whole of the time that God ordained. By deduction, therefore, we can conclude that no one sees anything unless it is allowed by God. Wow! Whilst the Egyptians lived for this time in utter darkness, this was not the case for the Israelites *who had light in the places where they lived*. God allowed this.

As I read these words the parallel for today stood out so clearly for me. Those who belong to the Lord, the ones who have surrendered to Him, live in the light. They are enlightened in the whole of their living, conditioned of course by the extent to which they will allow His light to guide them. The others, just like the Egyptians, will live in darkness. Perhaps the most striking difference between "the others" of today and the Egyptians of Moses' day is that the Egyptians knew they were in the darkness. The spiritual dark of today is much more subtle but every bit as dangerous and damaging.

Lord God,

May the light of Your Spirit shine strong and bright in the darkness that enshrouds much of this earth. I thank You that the light is on for me. My personal prayer is for more light – brighter and stronger. May Your light shine in me and my light shine in the world so that all may know that I am Yours.

I pray for others in whom Your light shines. Lord, may it shine more and more with each passing day. Strengthen Your saints and lead them into opportunities where they can victoriously minister Your love and saving grace.

I pray also for those who don't yet see Your light. Hear my cry and receive my prayer for them. Lord, soften hearts that have been hardened against You. I know it is Your heart to save the lost. I ask You to extend Your grace and draw these people into the light. Amen.

Partners

For we have become partners of Christ, if only we hold our first confidence firm to the end.

Heb. 3.14 NRSV

What a wonderful phrase is: **partners of Christ**. We are with Him, working with Him, at one with Him. We belong to Him and we participate in the many blessings that can only come in and through Him. Blessings, indeed, that abound in Him.

There is an "if only" for us. We must hold our first confidence firm to the end. Our first confidence comes with salvation. When we receive the Lord in those first days of new life and new creation, everything is almost too wonderful for words. We feel ten feet tall. We can do anything.

I take hold afresh of that confidence. Indeed: ***I can do everything through him who gives me strength*** (Phil. 4.13). That salvation I received so long ago hasn't left me. I am secure in it. And, in it, my confidence grows daily.

I am delighted to be a partner with Jesus. I look to His empowering anew, each and every day.

Lord God,

I thank You that You brought me into salvation. I thank You for the relationship I have with You and the partnership I share with Jesus.

Lord Jesus, I am confident in salvation and I receive anew and afresh the confidence I have in You. I ask You to fill me today with Your holy presence. It's You I cry out for, to fill me to overflowing.

Precious Lord, receive me today and lead me forward in partnership with You. I look forward to all that we are going to do together. Amen.

I lift up my soul

To you, O LORD, I lift up my soul; in you I trust, O my God.

Psalm 25.1, 2a

I see the soul as the centre and essence of my humanity. My mind and thinking, my heart and feeling locate in my soul. If I were not in relationship with God, then my life and my living would be driven by my soul.

However, as I am in relationship with God, it is important that I yield my soul to Him. To lift up my soul can be to hold up or give my soul to Him. It means surrender to Him. It means to worship Him.

I lift up my soul to Him as Lord. He is my guide and my ruler. He is my Master and I commit myself to listen to Him, to obey Him, to honour and respect Him.

As I lift my soul in honour and obedience to Him, I also put my trust in Him. I give Him my trust. I realise that this has been difficult for me. I'm not sure that this is yet fully achieved. I don't know how complete my trust is in God, but I do know that I want to reach that place of total trust in Him. He is my Maker and my Saviour. He is my Master and my Friend. He is Life itself to me. In Him I want to place my full confidence, my faith, and expectation.

Lord God,

I echo the words of the psalmist, but I also speak them anew and afresh – coming from my own mouth, expressing the desire of my heart.

To You, O Lord, I lift up my soul; in You I trust, O my God.

I look to You. I surrender to You. I give myself to You completely, and ask that You have Your way in me.

I bring more of the psalmist's words to You, as my own:

Guard my life and rescue me; let me not be put to shame, for

I take refuge in You. My integrity and uprightness protect me, because my hope is in You. Amen.

Faithful and True

I saw heaven standing open and there before me was a white horse, whose rider is called Faithful and True. With justice he judges and makes war.

Rev. 19.11

The King returns. And what a king! He is called Faithful and True. These descriptions are not too common in twenty-first century society. It is good to know they are not forgotten. In time, these words will overcome. The king will judge with justice. This is another word that is abused nowadays.

But, in time, truth will prevail. Meanwhile, even if society slips from faithfulness, truth, and justice, I do not need to abandon them.

I don't know when this king will return. Nor do I know what society in general will experience or what I in particular will have to live through. What I do know is that I need the king to get me through.

Lord God,

I salute the King of Heaven. I eagerly await your return in glory.

I pray that I may see Your glory even before You return to this earth. I pray also for Your presence always with me, giving me strength in every situation. There is much in society today that conflicts with Your truth and justice. I ask for wisdom, discernment, strength and boldness. I pray that I will know those issues I must respond to. I ask also for the right response. I do not want simply to generate hot air thereby achieving nothing. Neither do I want to remain silent if this is seen as acquiescing to what is not right by Your measure.

Guide me, great God, in paths of righteousness. Lead me to speak out, appropriately, as and when required. Help me to preserve the qualities of faithfulness, truth and justice in my life, and to touch those I come in contact with, with the same qualities. I ask this in Jesus' Name. Amen.

Be...

When Abram was ninety-nine years old, the LORD appeared to him and said, "I am God Almighty; walk before me and be blameless."

Gen. 17.1

Abram and Sarai had used a surrogate mother in their attempt to fulfil God's promise of offspring to them. It was not God's way. There is a clear lesson for me here. If God makes a promise He will fulfil it without any help or interference from me.

There is, however, something for me to do. As with Abram, God's faithful servant, I need to be obedient. Faith needs to be accompanied by the "obedience that comes from faith."

Abraham later demonstrated his obedience to God when asked to sacrifice his son Isaac.

When in a waiting pattern, it is difficult to know just how to be obedient to God. The human, and worldly, side of me feels that it must be doing. Even as I write this I sense God's reminder that He first wants me to **be**, and He will organise any doing. This is so alien to the ways of the world, and I struggle with it.

Still, it comes back to me, and with it comes reminders from God's Word:

Be still, and know that I am God

(Psalm 46.10).

...Mary has chosen what is better and it will not be taken away from her

(Luke 10.42).

Lord,

I confess that again I am restless. I want to be doing – for You.

*Today I am sensing a reminder for being rather than doing. Your Word requires obedience of me. I'm not exactly sure what that warrants at the present time. So I offer myself to You. I come to You and sit at Your feet. I wait upon You. If there is anything I am meant to **do**, I ask You to show me clearly. Meanwhile I will take each day as it comes, looking to You for all things, and resting in You at all times. Thank You for my life. Thank you for being with me. Amen.*

Appeal

Therefore, although in Christ I could be bold and order you to do what you ought to do, yet I appeal to you on the basis of love.

Philemon 8,9a

In this short entreaty to Philemon concerning his relationship with Onesimus, Paul wonderfully weaves the power of love into the fabric of forgiveness and everyday life. He feels entitled to order Philemon to receive back Onesimus and accept him, this time, as a brother and not as a slave. Instead of ordering, however, he appeals to Philemon on the basis of love.

I wonder how Philemon was feeling! Was Onesimus dispensable to him? Was he just another of many slaves? Or did he play a trusted role in Philemon's life? Would Philemon have been left greatly disheartened on the slave's desertion? And is this what indeed happened? We may conjecture at length all the possible circumstances behind this letter. And whatever we may wish to imagine as the outcome is also pure conjecture. Did Philemon heed Paul's appeal? Did he receive Onesimus back? And, if so, was it as a slave or as a brother? We may hope that the outcome was the sweet, good and Godly one.

But what do I receive from this incursion into these earlier Christian times? Essentially, two things! First, for me, there is the receiving. I may need correction at certain points in my Christian walk. I pray that God will communicate clearly with me at such times, either directly from Him to me, or by Him engaging a "Paul" to speak to me, to appeal to me in love. For my part, my prayer is that I will receive such advice, encouragement or rebuke totally in love and, in love, commit to following through.

The second insight is to do with giving. In giving, each time, my desire is to become more Christ-like. If I am ever called to speak encouragement or correction into anyone's life, may I to do so in the fullness of love. I pray for boldness, but a gentle boldness. Let me not order rudely in the name of Jesus. Let me, rather, minister in love and, even in rebuke, let encouragement be the mainstay of my ministry.

My Lord Jesus was not weak, but He was gentle. In His gentleness He was strong. He said, "Follow me." How I want to do this! I yearn to follow Him, to be like Him in so many ways. Today is a new day. God's mercies are new this morning. Today I am a new creation in Christ. Let me go forward with Him. Let me truly, "follow Him".

Lord God,

I come to You in feelings of overwhelming love. It bubbles up inside me. I want to let it out in a great big squeal of delight. I love You and I praise You for all You are doing in my life.

I thank You for today's insights through Paul and his writings. I take hold of the message that teaching and leading in love is more desirable and far more effective that living by legalism and by ordering people to do or not to do.

Gracious Father, I so want to follow the Son, to be like Him. I want to be strong and bold as He was. I want to be loving and gentle as He was. I want to be firm in resolve as He was. But, like Him, I say, "Yet not my will, but yours, be done."

I love you and want so much to share that love. Empower and lead me, in Jesus' Name I ask. Amen.

Wellspring of Life

Above all else, guard your heart, for it is the wellspring of life.

Prov. 4.23

I am prompted to look closely at two words that seem particularly relevant to the meaning and impact of this entreaty. The two words are "guard" and "wellspring'".

The heart is described as the wellspring of life. The Hebrew word that NIV translates "wellspring" is *tôtsâ'âh* (Strong, 8444) – *to-tsaw-aw'*. In this present context it connotes the source or place of "departure". In other words, the heart is the source of life, it is the place from which life originates or "departs" into the whole of our being and out into our environment and our world. Without the heart, we would have no life.

Clearly, we need to treat carefully this source of life. We need to "guard well" our hearts. The Hebrew word for guard is *nâtsar* (Strong, 5341) – *naw-tsar'*. It means to watch, to guard, and to keep. It implies faithfulness in the act – to faithfully watch and keep, to guard with diligence. And what should I watch, guard and keep? I believe I must carefully guard the source of life in me. I must watch that nothing damaging or impure touches my heart. I need to keep it constantly open to my Lord and God, to allow Him to have His way in me and in all that I do – at all times. If Jesus is truly my Lord, if He resides in me, then surely His place is my heart – the source, the origin of life itself. I want to keep this special place special for Him.

Lord,

I give You my heart. I desire to be Yours – wholly Yours – for all time. I will make it a priority to guard my heart, to watch what I allow to enter it, and to keep it for You.

Please help me Lord. I need to go forward in partnership with You. I need You in my heart, to fill my heart. Come, Lord, fill me. Lead me. Amen.

The Power in the Message

My message and my preaching were not with wise and persuasive words, but with a demonstration of the Spirit's power, so that your faith might not rest on men's wisdom, but on God's power.

1 Cor.2.4, 5

The preacher may not neglect adequate and proper preparation of his message for, as a custodian, deliverer and, maybe, interpreter of God's word, he has an obligation to be diligent and faithful.

But the words of the preacher will be of no good effect if the Holy Spirit is not at work in the hearts of the listeners.

The Spirit of God is given to us so that we may understand what is freely given by and from God (v12). The Spirit was promised by Jesus: *"But the Counsellor, the Holy Spirit, whom the Father will send in my name, will teach you all things and will remind you of everything I have said to you.*" (John 14.26)

The Spirit will both allow the speaker to bring spiritual words expressing spiritual truths and also allow the hearer to discern, receive and accept the spiritual truths spoken.

Paul tells us we have the mind of Christ (v16). I believe the Holy Spirit brings and unveils this to us.

Lord God,

I am so grateful for this, Your Holy Word, on a day when I am to speak to Your people. I pray that my preparation has been true, proper and acceptable. I ask You to take it and use it, and change it – and me – in the delivery if You so choose.

I ask You to move in the hearts of the listeners by the power of Your Holy Spirit, opening those hearts to receive Your spiritual truths through the words that come out of my mouth. I ask further that Your Holy Spirit will also move upon the listeners to respond in positive and delightfully accepting manner to the message and the growth that is available to them.

I ask this, humbly, in Jesus' name. Amen

Cease Striving

Be still and know that I am God;
I will be exalted among the nations,
I will be exalted in the earth.

Psalm 46.10

The New American Standard Bible (1997, p412) has "cease striving" for "be still". This reminds me of the day some time ago when I awoke to hear God say to me: "Stop striving."

I will not know God's power on this earth by striving to find it and to see it. God's might among the nations will be "revealed" to me as I am still and as I acknowledge the Almighty as all-mighty.

Mighty God,

I thank You for this reminder of who You are. I thank You that this has come to me in the stillness of the early morning. I truly feel as if I am not striving, yet I am aware of Your greatness.

I marvel as the light slowly reveals the day. The shadows disappear and Your creation is unveiled. The birds start singing. Are they the first to exalt You? Today is Sunday. All over the world people will be singing praises to You and glorifying Your name.

Great God, I bow down before you in worship and adoration. I declare You my Lord Almighty. Hallelujah! Amen.

Denial

As Simon Peter stood warming himself, he was asked, "You are not one of his disciples, are you?" He denied it, saying, "I am not."

John 18.25

Jesus had warned that Simon Peter would deny Him three times. Peter had protested. Yet when the time came he weakly denied his Lord and Saviour.

It is possible to be beguiled when reading the first part of this story to see oneself being strong where Peter was weak. Yet in reading the scene of the three denials one can readily see how they came about. After the first challenge "No, not me!" Then, "'fraid not." And finally, "No way!" And it's done. The Lord of Heaven is denied by mere man.

And so it goes on. Down through the ages humanity has denied Christ. Some, like Peter, have truly been followers, yet stumbled and mumbled when the challenge came. I think I have been like this. I repent and apologise to God and pray fervently that it will not happen again. Others don't even want to hear the gospel story. They dismiss Jesus as irrelevant and outdated. Perhaps these are fearful of what they perceive to be the price they have to pay. What these lost souls don't realise is that the price has already been paid, in full, by Him. We pay no price, we receive the benefit – the benefit of eternal life, begun already and lived each day as we commit to Him.

Certainly there are changes we make as we move from sin into salvation. But these changes do not bind or punish us. Personally I don't see them as punitive. Yes, we must "carry our cross" but this releases rather than restricts. In Jesus I find a freedom and a liberty that I do not find in the world. As I travel further with Jesus I am both relieved and delighted to shed the restrictions of worldly expectations. I am free and happy. I feel more "me" than ever I felt when trying to live by the world's distorted perspectives. I do not need to rise to any heights in worldly acclaim, dizzy or otherwise. The knowledge of who I am, who I truly am, is sufficient for me. I am a child of God and I am free to be me, truly me, totally me.

I do not realise the full extent of the character and being of my divine parent. For now, I know just enough to excite me, to sustain me, to encourage me, to animate me (O yes, I get so excited about God, and Jesus, and the Holy Spirit), and to lead me forward in an even greater expectation to see, to learn, to behold, to receive. My heavenly Dad is the most exciting. He can do anything. I say that, but I am slowly discovering the full extent of its meaning.

Yes, He can do anything and – guess what? I can do all things through Him who strengthens me. What a combination! What an amazing partnership!

Why would I ever want to deny this – to myself or to anyone else?

And why would anyone want to deny this wonderful and amazing opportunity – to join with the greatest force, to be family with God Almighty, to know this great, powerful, loving, forgiving, gracious being with the intimacy of the closest, deepest relationship – a real relationship, a meaningful connecting, and a powerful, profitable and fruitful partnership.

Amazing things can happen as we go forward with the One we were created to live in relationship with. We may witness, and be part of, world-changing events. We may see love spread across the face of the earth in an unprecedented outworking of the Father's will. We may see harmony between men and women, in neighbourhoods, in cities, and in nations. The will of God is that none shall perish but all might know eternal life.

Lord God,

Forgive me for those times when I have not acknowledged You as freely and as strongly as I should. Forgive me for those times when I may have denied You altogether. Forgive me and set me free. I pray that I will never again hold back from declaring You to be my Lord and Saviour. I want to loudly proclaim You. Help me, please.

I pray for those who know You but are uncertain of their belief. I pray for those who do not know You. I pray for the truth to be revealed and for the light of Jesus to shine clearly dispersing any darkness.

I pray for the world today. May those who know You willingly share their testimony, and Your love and grace, with all who will truly listen. I ask You to open ears to hear and eyes to see.

Come in power and undeniable love, in Jesus' name I ask. Amen.

God's plans

**O Lord, you are my God;
I will exalt you and praise your name,
for in perfect faithfulness you have done
marvellous things, things planned long ago.**

Isa. 25.1

As I read this I am reminded that God has a plan for my life. Furthermore, He made plans for me a long time ago, maybe even before time began. God is faithful, He is true in all that He does, and His long-standing plans for me will not be shelved or set aside. Whatever might intervene, and this includes any tardiness or failure on my part, God will have His way. His faithfulness is perfect – His Word tells me this. And the things that He planned for me so long ago will come to pass.

Today I am reassured that God has a plan for me. There is no detail about that plan. I am no more definite in this than I was yesterday, but I accept God's Word. He planned things for me a long time ago, things that are still to come to pass. In Him I have a hope and a future. He will show me the way. I must trust Him, rest in Him, and seek Him with all my heart.

Lord God,

I love You. I thank You for Your Word today. I take reassurance from You as I look to You for the way forward. Am I in the right place? Am I doing what You would have me do? Where would You have me? What would You have me do?

Great Guide, I look to You for direction and leading. I submit to You. Show me the way, in Jesus' name I ask. Amen.

Found

When he has found it, he lays it on his shoulders and rejoices.

Luke 15.5 NRSV

Jesus is telling the parables of salvation. His listeners comprise tax collectors and sinners, Pharisees and scribes – a mixed bag indeed. And His parables contained a mixture of personalities. Consider the prodigal family! The father – loving and kind, and rejoicing to see his son return; the elder son – hardworking, committed, but bitter and angry at the father's forgiving treatment of the repentant son; and then the younger son – brash, rash, fun-loving, foolish, awakened and then penitent. Indeed in one small family is found an amazing mix of raw material, potential for the kingdom of God.

But consider, not the variety of souls that are candidates for salvation, but rather the response that occurs at the moment of salvation.

Jesus compares the lost soul to the solitary sheep that wanders from the flock and finds itself lost and alone in the wilderness. The shepherd, in concern for this lost sheep, leaves the large flock to seek out the one lost. And when he finds it his response is most wonderful. We are told that he lays the sheep on his shoulders. In order to do this he must pick the sheep up. The shepherd finds the lost sheep, likely shivering, afraid and alone, and he picks it up. Imagine how comforting this would be for the sheep. He lays the sheep on his shoulders! Thus the sheep is safe, warm, and loved. The sheep is not forced to walk its own way back to the flock. Rather, it is carried. It is secure; it feels the warmth and care of the shepherd; it knows comfort and love. And the shepherd is filled with rejoicing.

And for every sinner saved there is great rejoicing in heaven – the great shepherd rejoices. When a lost soul finds the way, the Lord is filled with excitement. I can sense the excitement of heaven in the salvation of one lost soul. And heaven takes its lead from its leader. The Lord God, Father, Son and Spirit rejoice with the greatest delight at the return of the prodigal. The found-one is lifted upon the shoulders of the Saviour to find there rest and comfort, security and strength, peace, warmth and love. And from this close proximity to the source and the fountain of all love the found-one experiences intimately the Saviour's rejoicing. The shepherd has recovered the lost sheep, placed it lovingly on his caring shoulders, and carried it home – rejoicing. God be praised!

Lord God,

I thank You for the wonderful picture I receive from Your Word today. I see the great joy that is in all heaven when a lost sheep is found. But more than this I see Your absolute delight when one of Your beloved children returns to the fold.

O my Lord, I know there are many millions in this world who are lost. They are in the wilderness, and may not even know it. I cry out for them. I pray that representatives of the great shepherd are ever alert to the plight of the lost and are ever-willing to reach out, to seek, to care, and to lead into the arms of the Saviour.

I pray for the right response from those in the wilderness. I pray that the Holy Spirit might awaken the senses to know the reality of a lost existence. I pray for curiosity and enquiry

*after the truth for every lost soul. I pray for the truth to reach
beyond mere enquiry and curiosity and stir up a deep longing
for love.*

*I call out for Your grace, mercy and love. Salvation comes
from You. I ask You to release it, in greatest measure, over
these lost souls, in Jesus' name. Amen.*

God delivers

**"They will pass through the sea of trouble;
the surging sea will be subdued and all the depths of
the Nile will dry up.
Assyria's pride will be brought down and Egypt's
sceptre will pass away.
I will strengthen them in the LORD and in his name
they will walk," declares the LORD.**

Zech. 10.11,12

God is talking about delivering His people out of exile. Egypt and
Assyria both would have evoked strong memories of slavery and
exile for the Jews.

God states that His people will pass through this trouble, the
threatening seas that surge around them will be subdued, and the
menacing waters of the Nile will dry up. The power and might
of the oppressors will be removed and God will strengthen His
people in Himself. They will walk in Him.

This is God's declaration for His people. He spoke it out
clearly for the exiled remnant of Jews. But I believe He speaks it
just as clearly today. Many of Christ's followers are threatened – by
all manner of affliction in many different situations. The forces
of evil that exerted such influence through Assyria and Egypt

are equally at work today. Their environment is of now, their manner and persuasion is totally contemporary in every respect. Yet as we read of God's deliverance of His people from their old-time foes we do not readily transpose it into today's society. This, however, does not deny it. God will save His people today. His rescue operation is underway for all who will turn to Him, and heed Him.

The strength we receive in Him will lead us through any conflict. In Him, we are secure; we find the will to fight the poor and pathetic ways of the enemy, demonstrated through a fallen world. We are lifted up and restored into wonderful relationship where we can walk fully in Him.

Father God,

I pray for Your children who are struggling today. I know, like any parent, You are concerned for them; Your desire is to help and protect, save and strengthen.

Great God, Wonderful Dad, I cry out for the lost. Those who are so enmeshed and deceived by 'Egypt' and 'Assyria' that they can't take hold of You with any strength, or sense of reality. Lord, would You reach out to them? Would You hold them in peace, in the palm of Your hand? Let them notice the stillness. Let them feel the peace. Let them know that the hand of Almighty God, their loving, heavenly Father is on them, to strengthen them and lead them from the grip of the enemy.

Lord God, I thank You for each and every human being on the face of this earth. Reach them, and save them, in Jesus' name I ask. Amen.

"Come"

"Lord, if it's you," Peter replied, "tell me to come to you on the water."
"Come," he said.
Then Peter got down out of the boat, walked on the water and came toward Jesus. But when he saw the wind, he was afraid and, beginning to sink, cried out, "Lord, save me!"

Matt.14. 28-30

I see an interesting aspect to this narrative as I read it today. It seems to me that Peter has something he wants to do. In the natural what he wants is impossible, but he seems to understand that all things are possible with God (expressed later by Matthew in 19.26). He knows that if Jesus is in it, his desire will eventuate. The way of knowing whether Jesus is for this hare-brained scheme or not is to ask. How simple!

Peter asks, and Jesus responds. **"Come"** he says. He is effectively saying, **"Yes, I am in this with you. I am for you and I will be with you as you trust in me."**

Peter hears what Jesus says and responds. Initially he does well. But then he looks to the natural environment around him. It is as though he forgets the encouraging "Come" of Jesus. Perhaps he takes his eyes off Jesus. Maybe, he suddenly sees himself operating in his own strength and realises his own inadequacy.

Of course, the story ends for Peter with Jesus coming to the rescue.

I'm quite amused that Peter is the particular disciple featured in this adventure. Even as I have written his name in this reflection, I see myself in his place. And perhaps, just maybe, God is speaking to me today through my illustrious namesake. And what might He be saying? What I think I'm hearing is something like this:

"Peter, it's alright to think about what you'd like to do for me. You don't have to wait until it drops out of the heavens. No, please open your mind to the limitless possibilities. Dream, and don't be afraid to dream big. Remember, nothing – absolutely nothing – is impossible with me. When you're in that very special place of resting, abiding in me, let your mind embrace all and every scenario. Remember, always remember, that I am for you.

When you dream, don't leave it at that, but be willing to share your dreams with me. Let me in. I so want you to include me in your dreaming and vision making. Share with me and invite me to lead you. Allow me to say "Come". But when I do, I ask for your complete trust. I ask you to look to me, fully and steadfastly, unwaveringly and constantly – and that means at all times and in every situation. Keep your eyes fixed on me and do not be tempted, like the earlier Peter, to look on the prevailing natural circumstance or situation, for these will surely put you off and cause you to falter. I need your full trust. Your confidence is to be placed totally in me, in who I am and what I can do, in who you are in me and what I can do through you. Now consider, reflect, and share your dreams with me. Come."

Dear Lord and Father,

I thank You for these words today which, in a sense, have come literally "out of the blue". Indeed, even when I started to pen what I thought You might be saying, I had no idea what would eventuate. I sense, and believe, that You have truly and clearly spoken to me today. Thank You for what You have said. It is timely but, then, isn't that Your perfect way?

111

I think I have held back a little up until now. Certainly I have been in touch with dreams and aware of certain desires, but I have tended to say 'God knows' and then to leave the initiative to You. Are You, today, asking for more expression from me? Well, I don't have a clear and concise thesis to present to You but perhaps I can start to express something of my dreams and desires. Maybe this will lead to further expression or additions at future times.

I believe You once gave me an exhortation to "Tell my people I love them." I receive this. I want to share, not just the message, but also the reality of Your love. Whilst I am available for whatever You would have of me, I am drawn, strangely yet I think intentionally, to those who are already in the community of believers. I would dearly love to minister more to the needs within the family, to pastors, leaders and their families, to be a listening ear and a compassionate voice, maybe a sounding board and reference point, and to offer practical help and assistance where appropriate.

I have a heart for the universal church of Jesus Christ. In this church I see no barriers of denomination or doctrinal differences. I simply see Your precious children and I see the needs that many, if not all, have. I know I cannot achieve these things in my own resources. This would certainly be a case where Jesus would need to say "Come".

But I realise I need to work without restriction, to release myself fully to You without any reserve. I withdraw all conditions or descriptions of any kind. I release myself totally into Your will, trusting You with absolutely all of my being.

Dear Holy Father, I offer to You my dreams and aspirations, my love and caring for people, for all people but, especially, for those within the community of believers. I offer also to You myself – my life, my heart, my being. Let me say,

*Lord if this is your will or whatever might be Your will, show
me and invite me to come.*

*And, may I be willing.I pray this sincerely and earnestly,
in Jesus' Name. Amen.*

Ask!

**The men of Israel sampled their provisions but did not
inquire of the LORD.**

Joshua 9.14

The Gibeonites sought to deceive the Israelites by claiming to come
from a far country to seek a treaty, thereby avoiding extermination.
God had told the Israelites to take the whole of the Promised Land
and to leave no survivors. To comply with this, the Israelites would
have needed to know that the Gibeonites were not who they said
they were, and then to have destroyed them. The immediate action
for the Israelites would have been to check out the Gibeonites story
with the Lord.

However, when the Gibeonites gave their story, the Israelites
listened, but did not enquire of the Lord. A grave mistake was
made, for which the Israelites were later to pay.

We also need to enquire of God when major decisions are
to be made. We cannot presume any action. A simple request to
God will yield the guidance we need, and an inner peace will
confirm it.

Lord God,

*I thank You for the lesson I see today in the story of the
Israelites reaction to the story of the Gibeonites. I pray that I
may never may such a mistake.*

*I thank You that You are always there to lead and direct
me. I repent for those times when I have not enquired of You,
and I ask Your forgiveness.*

I pray Your guidance in all of my life, in every decision and action, in Jesus' name. Amen.

Heavenly Wisdom

But the wisdom that comes from heaven is first of all pure; then peace-loving, considerate, submissive, full of mercy and good fruit, impartial and sincere.

James 3.17

James has already (1.5) encouraged his readers to ask God if they lack wisdom and God will give wisdom **generously to all without finding fault**. He now tells us some of the qualities of the wisdom that God gives. Firstly, it is pure – untainted and unadulterated. It is strong and totally Godly. It looks for peace. Wisdom, true wisdom, knows the folly of disagreement. Disagreements can lead to war. Wisdom, then, will work out disagreement and seek to make peace. It may make such peace, a peace that is just and acceptable to all parties in a dispute. Peace-making is not peace-keeping. Peace-keeping often has a price. Peace-making calls for no such penalty but brings liberation in full.

Wisdom is considerate. It does not dismiss any idea or party out of hand. Wisdom will gently, but firmly, deal with offence. It will be considerate in its hearings, and in its resolutions. Wisdom is submissive. What might James mean by this? I believe he means that wisdom will not vaunt itself nor lord it over situations. Neither will wisdom be downtrodden. Rather, perhaps in meekness, it will work – again gently but firmly.

Wisdom is full of mercy. What a wonderful, and necessary, characteristic! Mercy is an indicator of true love. Wisdom is also full of good fruit. This is worth remembering. Where heavenly wisdom is exercised no bad fruit will result. Wisdom is impartial.

It does not take sides. It listens attentively to all arguments and contributes in mercy and consideration, seeking peace and expecting good fruit.

Wisdom is sincere. There is no pretence with wisdom. The truly wise are not hypocritical. No "acting" is required with wisdom. It is genuine. It is real. It is sincere.

What a wonderful gift God's wisdom is!

Lord God,

I rejoice in the qualities that pertain to the wisdom You give. James tells me that if I lack wisdom I should ask You for it. I may have some wisdom which, I'm sure, is from You. But I know I could use much more. And so I ask for it. I ask, knowing that as You grant it to me it will come in purity, peace-loving, considerate, submissive, full of mercy and good fruit, impartial and sincere. I look forward to this. I thank You for this precious gift.

I ask also for opportunities to make peace, sowing in peace and knowing that I will raise a harvest of righteousness.

I thank You. I love You. I bless You. Amen.

How Deep?

The word of the LORD came to me: "Go and proclaim in the hearing of Jerusalem: 'I remember the devotion of your youth, how as a bride you loved me and followed me through the desert, through a land not sown.'"

Jer. 2.1,2

These beautiful words of affirmation of Israel are soon to be followed by God's question, **"What fault did your fathers find in me, that they strayed so far from me?"** (v5) In her youth, Israel was devoted to the Lord. She loved Him as a bride, and willingly followed Him through desert territories knowing that He held good in store for her. But, just as the love of some brides wanes and turns sour, so Israel relapsed and strayed far from God.

This stirs me up with the question today being: Am I as deeply and fully in love with God, and as totally devoted to Him as I have ever been?

I can say, "I want to be!" I can acknowledge, "I need to be!" But, am I? Could I now follow God through the desert? Can I trust him to lead me, whether it be into a land of milk and honey or – wherever? Or would I rather say, "Where are You, Lord? Why have You left me?"

The issue is not where God is, but where I am.

Lord God, Sweet Jesus,

My desire is to love You more and to be more totally committed to You today than I have ever been. My wish is that our relationship will be closer and stronger and deeper tomorrow than it is today. And so on.

I seek a new outpouring of Your Holy Spirit in my life that will bring me into deeper intimacy with You.

O Lord, hear my prayer. Amen.

Remain

"Remain in me, and I will remain in you."

John 15.4a

In chapter 15 of his gospel, John presents Jesus telling His disciples that He is the vine and the Father is the gardener. He further tells us that His disciples, we, are the branches of the vine. The Father/gardener will prune the vine, cutting off every branch that bears no fruit. Jesus then records that no branch can bear fruit by itself; it must remain in the vine. Similarly we will bear no fruit unless we remain in Him. As we remain in Him, so He will remain in us.

I am conscious of the order in this sentence. Jesus asks me first to remain in Him. Then He will remain in me. It is my choice to remain in Jesus. And my action must follow through with my choice.

I can choose to say, "When I've finished this, I'll remain in You." Or, "When this is done, I'll come to You." Or even, "In a minute or two, I'll be with You." Or I can choose to say, "Lord, here I am right now."

Lord Jesus,

I find that there may always be distractions that will seek to keep me from You. I choose to ignore the distractions. I choose You. I say, "Lord, here I am. Take me."

Take me, Lord, and make me Your own. Do what You will with me. Let me have no desire other than to do Your will for my life, Your full and perfect will.

I come to You. I want nothing else. Take me. Let me abide in You. Abide in me, Lord, in Your precious name I ask. Amen.

Rain in the Desert

The boy Samuel ministered before the LORD under Eli. In those days the word of the LORD was rare; there were not many visions.

1 Sam. 3.1

We are told that God rarely spoke in these times. It seems that the Israelites had been in a spiritual desert for some time.

Indeed, when God spoke to Samuel, for the first three times, Samuel thought that it was Eli who had called him. He presented himself to Eli in response. The narrative tells us: ***Now Samuel did not yet know the LORD. The word of the LORD had not yet been revealed to him.*** (v7)

It was Eli who, after the third call, realised that it was the LORD who was calling the boy. At the fourth call, therefore, Samuel was able to respond, ***"Speak, for your sevant is listening."*** (v10)

God spoke at length to Samuel, throughout his long ministry. And He told him amazing things.

Even in times of apparent drought God can release rain.

Lord God,

You chose to break the spiritual drought that the Israelites experienced for so long. I praise You for this.

I rejoice that You speak to me. I thank You for the words – Your Word – that You have communicated to me in the past. I open myself up for Your leading in the future. May I, like Samuel respond, saying "Speak, for Your servant is listening."

I cherish Your Word. I pray for greater insight into Your Word and further opportunities to share it with others. I thank You for the abundant life that is in Your Word.

Hallelujah! Glory to You, Lord. I praise Your name. I lift You up in the highest. May Your rain continue to fall. Amen.

More and more

Finally, brothers, we instructed you how to live in order to please God, as in fact you are living. Now we ask you and urge you in the Lord Jesus to do this more and more...

And in fact, you do love all the brothers throughout Macedonia. Yet we urge you, brothers, to do so more and more.

1 Thess. 4.1, 10

These two verses convey a common truth to me. It's more than the expression "more and more", yet this is the key to it. Paul talks of living in order to please God. He also talks of loving **all the brothers**, surely an act which is pleasing to God. We are strongly exhorted to live in the fullness of pleasing God loving, not only the Holy Trinity but, all of humanity too. And we are to do this **more and more.**

These three words bring excitement into my spirit. They indicate to me that I am on a journey, and I have further to go. This encourages and delights me. I realise that I am not already there. I can happily say, "I'm glad this is not it!" I can, also happily, look forward to **more and more**. There may be more and more challenges but there will also be more and more grace. For surely, **where sin increased, grace increased all the more** (Rom. 5.20). I may be called to endure more and more hardship, to experience more and more suffering and disappointment. But if I press in to God and seek Him always, I may know Him more and more intimately. I will, hopefully, become more and more Christ-like.

I rejoice in the knowledge – in the clear and joyful knowing – that I am a son of my heavenly Father. I know there are times when I struggle but, if I will only remember it, He is right there with me.

I delight that the journey continues. Jesus has said to me, "Follow me." I eagerly follow Him, reminding myself, when the going gets tough, of all that He endured for me. Indeed I can honestly say, even in the direst of times, "Well, Lord, they haven't yet done to me what they did to You." He is my example, my guide and my mentor. In response to His invitation I say, "Lord Jesus, I come."

Lord God,

I thank You first of all for a new day and the newness of life that is in me. I thank You for the love You have for me that led You to give Your very self in divine sacrifice so that I might be reunited with You. In You I am freed of the shackles of sin. I know You in intimacy and I have the assurance of eternal blessing. I thank You that I do not have to wait for this wonderful life in You, for it has already begun.

I thank You also for the glorious invitation from my Lord Jesus to follow Him. I am not worthy, Lord. I know this and You know this. Yet it doesn't matter. You accept me as I am, but You love me too much to allow me to remain as I am.

*I come to You, and I ask for more. Lord, I ask for more and more of Your love. I ask for more and more healing, teaching, guiding, equipping and fulfilling. May I know the fullness of Christ in me. Yes, Lord, please fill me, **as full as is absolutely possible**, with the real and dynamic presence of Jesus in me. Lead me to live to fully please You. Let me love every brother and sister beyond measure. And may I do these things 'more and more' as I ask it in Jesus' name. Amen.*

God of the Dark

As the sun was setting, Abram fell into a deep sleep, and a thick and dreadful darkness came over him.

Gen. 15.12

How often do we fear darkness? We so readily jump to conclusions of spiritual darkness – God is not with us! God has abandoned us!

God spoke to Abram through the darkness. He told him amazing things about his own destiny and also that of his people. He told him of trial and tribulations that were to come upon his people. But it was also out of the darkness that God gave Abram the covenant promise that was to lead to God's amazing provision for his people. The darkness was a time for Abraham to listen. God was most certainly not absent in the darkness.

Oswald Chambers (1927, p.25) says: Whenever God gives a vision to a saint, He puts him, as it were, in the shadow of His hand, and the saint's duty is to be still and listen. There is a darkness which comes from excess of light, and then it is time to listen.

Abram sets a good example.

When darkness falls, it could be just the time for me to give myself over completely to God, to be present for Him, to listen attentively to what He might say, and to be willing to carry through on anything He may ask of me.

Lord God,

I pray that I may never fear darkness. I pray that I may see it as an excess of light in its origin. I pray that I might know, in darkness that I am in the shadow of Your hand.

I pray that darkness will encourage me to be still, and listen to You. This is my prayer. Amen.

The greatest

But they kept quiet because on the way they had argued about who was the greatest.

Mark 9.34

It seems that status and self-importance were around even in Jewish religious society of two thousand years ago. I wonder if it was as infectious as it is today!

The disciples had been arguing about rank and status yet they kept quiet when questioned by Jesus. They likely knew that such self-focused concerns had no place in Jesus' value system. But were they prepared for His response? – *"If anyone wants to be first, he must be the very last, and the servant of all"* (v. 35).

Not only does He ignore rank and status, He actually advocates the opposite – becoming *servant of all.* Of course, this is what He went on to prove. And He exhorts His disciples – that is, every sincere believer – to *"Follow me."*

Do these words bring comfort, or challenge? I receive them. I will try my utmost to live by them. As I do so, I remind myself of further words of Jesus: *"And surely I am with you always, to the very end of the age"* (Matt. 28.20). Hallelujah!

Lord God,

I truly want to be a servant in Your service. I know I will not achieve this in my own strength. So I call on You.

Receive me into Your greater service. Enable me with divine wisdom; empower me with Your Holy Spirit. Fill me with the love of God and the peace of Jesus, and use me in the fullness of Your will.

Let me be ever alert for opportunities to serve You. Give me the thoughts to think, the words to speak and the actions to follow.

*Let me **never** be tempted to seek position or status. I do
not see these as of Your Kingdom. May I rather know the
contentment that Paul knew – whatever the circumstance.
I would willingly come last if I am allowed to follow Jesus.
I offer this prayer in His precious name. Amen.*

Thirst assuaged

**My soul thirsts for God, for the living God.
When can I go and meet with God?**

Psalm 42.2

The psalmist sounds desperate in his cry to meet with the living
God. Apparently something is afflicting him which is preventing
him from attending the temple, where he might meet with his God.

How blessed I am that I do not need to attend any specific
place to meet with God. I know He is with me right now, here
on my sunny verandah, even as the power tools drone on the
neighbour's renovations site. God is here. I am with Him. My
thirst is being assuaged. I am at peace.

I no longer need a temple, or a priest, to assure me of God's
presence, to affirm that my prayers are heard. My Lord Jesus has
made it possible, for all time, for me to enter into communion
and intimacy with my Lord and my God in the case of every
environment and every situation. I do not take this lightly. I
respect and appreciate my Lord's sacrifice. I receive and enjoy the
privilege. I thank my God for His wonderful grace.

*Lord God,
I thank You for the amazing privilege of being Your child.
Right now I feel Your presence. I sense an overwhelming move*

of peace and power. The workmen's tools are silent, the breeze is gentle and the birds chirp happily. You are here.

In this mildest of autumn weather, the sun is still bright in the sky. The evidence of Your presence is all around me. But, right now, the strongest evidence is within me. I "feel" You're here. I sense Your security covering me. I am truly "at home" for I am where I belong – resting in You.

I seek to abide in You at all times. I ask You to lead me through this day. Have Your way in what I do, who I meet, where I go. I love You, Lord. Receive my love; receive me, in Jesus' Name I ask. Amen.

Suddenly

Suddenly Jesus met them. "Greetings," he said. They came to him, clasped his feet and worshipped him.

Matt. 28.9

This brief cameo, from the events of the day of Resurrection illustrates the whole experience of Resurrection life in Jesus.

The unbeliever may suddenly experience an encounter with the living Christ. Life may be progressing in routine way, perhaps even in gloom as I sense the women felt on that first Easter morning. But, when they met with Jesus, any misery was dispelled. Their Lord was with them, truly with them this time, for He had conquered sin and death and was positively placed to lead them into the fullness of renewed relationship with God.

Suddenly He met them. God works often in the suddenlies. The women were likely in the depths of despair, grief and mourning and – suddenly – Jesus is there. But, more than this, he **met** them. An encounter with Jesus happens when **He** meets us. We may have searched. We may have made many attempts to draw near, to press in, but the action that saves proceeds from Him. It is when He determines the time is right that we might experience a suddenly. And, suddenly, all manner of things begin to fall into the right place.

We may seek and search, and this is good but, in the end, He finds us. He will meet us and maybe, like the women, we know that we are ready to meet Him. The women had come to the tomb looking for Jesus. We may, or may not, be aware that we are seeking, that we are earnestly looking out for Him. We can believe that He seeks us out for He himself said, the Father **seeks** those who will worship Him in spirit and truth (John 4.23).

When He meets with us, He calls to us in greeting. He invites us into relationship. Each time we encounter Him, He says "Greetings". He is always ready to welcome us, to receive us, to acknowledge us and to join with us. He reminds us that we did not choose Him, but He chose us (John 15.16). This is true, yet we have the option of coming to Him or not. I see this as perhaps the weightiest exercise of any option there might be. He comes to us, maybe suddenly. He meets with us and extends greetings to us. He is inviting us to respond. We may turn away, or we may come to Him. Oh, that we might respond positively to His invitation!

Lord God,

I rejoice in this revelation of Your wonderful working. I thank You for this insight into the experience of the women on the day of Resurrection. I thank You that this same experience is available to all whom You choose and invite to respond to You, and for the reminder that Jesus welcomes us with loving greeting each and every time we turn to Him.

Lord, I pray for the countless unsaved on the face of the earth. I pray for a glorious season of suddenlies. I ask for the faith to believe that Your saving power will bring many that

I know and love into true and lasting relationship with You.
I ask these things in Jesus' name. Amen.

Wisdom

The quiet words of the wise are more to be heeded than the shouts of a ruler of fools. Wisdom is better than weapons of war, but one sinner destroys much good.
Eccles. 9.17,18

Words from a wise man's mouth are gracious, but a fool is consumed by his own lips.
Eccles. 10.12

Wisdom is surely a gift from God. It is a most powerful gift. We are told how effective quiet words of wisdom are. Wisdom does not need to be loud and abusive. This is the way of a ruler of fools. Wisdom is quiet, true and effective. Wisdom is gracious. The wise man does not exercise his own ego. He graciously imparts insight and understanding. He will not speak for the sake of hearing his own voice. His speech will guide others, and he will share humbly and without fanfare.

Wisdom will overcome more strife than warring will. Wisdom is a mighty weapon in the fight for truth. Sin is destructive. Wisdom can release from sin, and lead the sinner in the right ways.

I am encouraged that sin cannot deny a person the walk of righteousness.

There is not a righteous man on earth who does what is right and never sins.
Eccles. 7.20

Lord God,

I am a sinner and I humbly acknowledge my sin before You. I confess and repent and seek Your forgiveness.

I seek wisdom. I ask for God-given wisdom. I pray that I might help those who struggle with life's problems. I want to help them and share God's way with them. Would You allow me to do this by an impartation of wisdom?

I pray also for a gracious disposition. In Your grace, Lord, impart grace into me.

Take me forward into this day, into this world, to impart Your grace and wisdom to the needy, in Jesus' name I ask. Amen.

Stand firm

So, if you think you are standing firm, be careful that you don't fall.

1 Cor. 10.12

This is a worthy warning to bear in mind at all times, indeed, to live by.

I may think I am standing firm. I might feel most secure in God, yet I must be ever alert. There is no room for complacency in the Christian life. I need always to be on guard against the attacks of the enemy. And the more I seem to grow and prosper in Christ, the greater the threat I become to Satan and the bigger a target for his fiery darts.

Paul continues his writing and tells me that any temptation I experience is also known to others. There is no original temptation. All have been used before in devilish manipulation.

But God is faithful. He is faithful and He will not allow the temptation to go beyond my capacity to bear it. When I am faced with temptation God will provide a way out. He will enable me to stand up under temptation and to overcome it.

Yet, I must be diligent. Surely I need to keep my eyes fixed firmly on God. Temptation is often appealing, but I don't think it is all that subtle. If I remain alert, I can generally discern when temptation rears its ugly head. And this is when I take action. I act immediately and my first move is to turn to God, to turn fully to Him, and to turn the temptation over to His holy response. If I waver, I could be lost. I cannot afford to give any recognition or measure to the ways of sin. James urges me to: **Resist the devil, and he will flee from you** (Jas. 4.7). What a great thing it is to spurn Satan, to be able to turn from him knowing that we can so wonderfully walk with a loving Father who both protects us and blesses us. The ways of the Lord are the ways I want to embrace with the whole of my being. There is none like Him. I want to abide in Him always, to walk and talk with Him, to live and move and have my being in Him. Hallelujah!

Lord God, Heavenly Father,

There are sinful ways and desires of the flesh that I know would seek to draw me from You. I do not want this, and so I lay these things before You. I seek Your forgiveness, Your protection against any evil thing that might seek to assail me, and Your leading in right ways.

I am no different to other men. The temptations that seek to provoke me assail others to. But I do not want to succumb.

Holy, Heavenly Father, hear my prayer. Receive my cry for greater union and deeper intimacy with You. Receive it, and answer it, please.

Show me your ways clearly. Strengthen me and guide me to walk always in them. I love you. I would share this love with others. Freely I have received from You. Let me freely share. Amen.

Little by little

*Little by little I will drive them out before you, until you
have increased enough to take possession of the land.*

Exodus 23.30

God is unfolding His plan for the Israelites. He has promised
them a land flowing with milk and honey where they are to live
in total possession. **All** of the present inhabitants are to be driven
out so that there is no obstruction and no sharing of what God has
promised and reserved for His chosen people. But the whole task
is a big one and will not be accomplished in one single activity.
God says, *"I will not drive them out in a single year, because
the land would become desolate and the wild animals too
numerous for you."* (v.29)

God's plan is progressive. It is clear, and here He clearly presents
it to His people. What He requires of them is their obedience to
what He asks of them. Sadly, a look at the continuing story of the
Israelites will show that they were not always obedient and thus
missed out on the fullness of God's plan for them.

I am reminded of the immutability of God. He is never-
changing, the same always.

His plan for me may quite well mirror the plan He had for
the Israelites – certainly in its outworking. He will uncover His
promises for me, little by little. He knows that if He were to
declare it all in one revelation it would be too much for me to
receive. Also, I would be in no way ready or prepared to receive it.

No, the timing is God's. He reveals in His time, at His pace,
and in full accord with His plan. And His expectation of me is just
what He expected of Moses and His people – obedience.

This is sometimes so very hard. There are times when I feel
that God has "lost the plot" in terms of His purposes for me. There
are times of impatience. "Why are we waiting? Surely I'm ready

right now!" There can't possibly be more preparation necessary, more clearing and feeding of the soil. Or can there? Do I need to increase some more in Him? I am slowly recognising that God knows best. I hope I am growing in grace such that I can truly say, "Your will not mine be done", and I can say it in humility and sincerity. May I also graciously wait upon God when He seems to be dragging the chain or to have forgotten the urgency of our quest.

My life in Him depends totally upon His grace. I pray for an outpouring of that grace to enable me to live every moment in a state of gracious rest in Him, truly saying, "Not what I want, but what You want."

Holy Father, Dearest Lord,

I sense Your peace at this moment and I am able, for the present at least, to say that Your plan is clearly unfolding in my life and I am at ease with its timing and rate of progress.

I ask You to forgive me for the times, the many times, when I am impatient for the plan to unfold. At such times, I guess, I'm looking to my agenda and not Yours. Please forgive me. I truly want to go Your way, in all that I do. I want to be so lost in You that I would be totally at sea in any situation where I am not fully led by You.

You are my life. I rejoice that You have drawn me to You. I thank You for the sweet relationship I have with You. And I ask for more. I yearn to go deeper, to draw nearer, and to come closer. Hear my prayer, Lord, and, if it moves Your heart, then draw me so close that I might hear Your heartbeat, and live in perfect harmony with it.

I am willing to go wherever You would have me go. I will do whatever You want me to do. But only if You go with me and You guide and support me. I am nothing without

*You. Oh, I praise You, Lord. I thank You for this wonderful
revelation which moves me to seek You in everything.*

*I seek, and I find. I rejoice, and I am greatly encouraged
to seek more. May this never stop. Lead me through this day,
and the whole of my life. Let me journey everywhere with
You, in Jesus' name I ask. Amen.*

All

**Calling his disciples to him, Jesus said, "I tell you the
truth, this poor widow has put more into the treasury
than all the others. They all gave out of their wealth;
but she, out of her poverty, put in everything – all she
had to live on."**

Mark 12.43, 44

Jesus asks for my all. I like to think that I am willing in this, yet
I sometimes wonder. The story of the poor widow is a startling
reminder. This dear soul gave all she had.

It is interesting that Mark first notes the large amounts that
the rich people put into the temple treasury. Yet, at the end of the
day, they were still rich. The widow, on the other hand, gave all
her worldly means – and was left with nothing. Nothing, that is,
of herself or what the world could give her. The rich presumably
continued with life, looking to their own means for support and
provision. The widow had no means left. She had emptied herself
fully of herself and her hope of self-provision. Now she was totally
available. God could now come into her life in divine majesty and
splendour and endow her, as He pleased, with the riches of heaven.

There is really no comparison between the self-preserving rich
of this story and the all-sacrificing poor widow. How do I fare in
this scheme?

Lord God,

I want to serve You with all of my being, to surrender my all to You, yet I am greatly apprehensive of losing the necessities for living. I try not to hold on, but I don't always succeed in letting go.

I commit to You anew. I will myself to surrender. Take me, Lord, and make me Yours. Help me when I struggle to hold on. You are my provider. I know this and I thank You. Let me give myself into Your provision, trusting You for all that I need and allowing You to have Your way in me.

Receive me, Lord. Lead me. I want to go the way You would have me go, the way that is totally pleasing to You. Hallelujah! Amen.

Foreseeing...?

But God sent me ahead of you to preserve for you a remnant on earth and to save your lives by a great deliverance.

Gen. 45.7

These words carry the substance of great prophecy. Was Joseph in fact foreseeing the great deliverance of God's people through the exodus from Egypt?

Another major theme that he hints at in these few, almost careless, words is the remnant. I'm not sure if this is the first mention, yet it is extremely potent.

Joseph sees clearly that it is by God's plan that he is in Egypt. He also sees God's plan embracing two specific events – the preservation of a remnant, and the occurrence of a great deliverance. We see, from a place of retrospection, the enormous significance of both these themes for the whole people of God, first the Israelites/ Jews and then the Christians.

I am in wonderment of the enormity of God and the intricacy of His design and its outworking. In what appears disastrous in some respects, God meant Joseph's life and his varied experiences for good. I can see how this good was not simply for Joseph and his family but, indeed, for the whole of humanity.

Lord God,

You are truly wonderful beyond any comparison. I exalt and magnify You. I praise and worship You to the highest heavens.

I see, whether correctly or simply imaginatively, how Your plan for Joseph has had such a far reaching effect. I believe this is Your way. You work in each of us not only for our own good but also for the benefit of others.

I submit myself to the fullness of Your plan for me. I pray Your purpose is to touch and help many through Your working in my life. I surrender and give myself to Your way, in the glorious name of Jesus. Amen.

Great love

But because of his great love for us, God, who is rich in mercy, made us alive with Christ even when we were dead in transgressions – it is by grace you have been saved.

Eph. 2.4, 5

The first thing this Scripture tells me is that God loves me, and His love for me is great. Right now, I need to hear this. I feel low in spirit, side-lined by God, and not being used by him according to the desire I have for Him to use me.

Yet, even as I write these words, my mind sees through them. My mind says, 'But surely it's not what you want, but what God wants. And, as you so often cry out to God for His will to be done in your life, so you need to accept, at this very moment, that you are precisely in His will for this time. His will is to occasion no more "doing" from you than the little that is happening.' This is most interesting self-talk. I remind myself to listen carefully, for it is as if God is speaking to me through myself.

These verses tell me more than God loves me. They also tell me that, through His rich mercy, He made me alive in Christ even whilst I transgressed. The reality is that I am still in transgressions, yet He makes me alive in Christ. Minute by minute He brings me to life, in Christ. And this is purely and simply by His grace.

I see here a difference between reality and truth. My present reality is that of a "downer". I feel despondent and could easily chuck it all in. Yet I am stopped simply because I don't know what that means. Chuck in what? And chuck it into – where? I think what I'm saying is that I'm ready to stop trying and sink into an abyss of self-pity. This appears as the present reality. But the truth is vastly different. And the truth breaks forth today in God's very words to me. He loves me. His love for me is **great**! And in His mercy He brings me to life. I live in His love, and I live in Jesus. I feel my spirit rise. Again the self-talk comes and says, "How dare you feel down and low in the face of such love and mercy and abundant grace, that has saved you (yes, I do know this!) and now, this very moment, brings you to life and fills you with the very fullness of Christ."

Lord God,

First I say sorry. I'm sorry for forgetting that I am a much loved child of the most wonderful God. I'm sorry that I allow myself to give in to doubt and despair, and even to indulge in self-pity. Please forgive me. You are my all. I thank You for the love, mercy and grace that brought me to salvation in Christ. Paul reminds me of the faith that occasioned this. And this faith was not of my doing, but was a gift from You.

*My Dear Father, I dare to ask for Your gift of further faith. I ask also for infilling, and constant topping-up, with the fullness of Christ in me. Let me be **always** aware, every second of every day, of Your presence with me. I will say, with Moses, if You don't go with me, I don't want to go. Come with me today. Dear Lord, lead me on, in Jesus' name I ask. Amen.*

Forgiving... and remaining

Be kind and compassionate to one another, forgiving each other, just as in Christ God forgave you.

Eph. 4.32

We have been forgiven in Christ. This is the fundamental truth of Christian living. We are sinners who have been forgiven. And we are invited, nay exhorted, to follow Christ. We need to forgive, freely and without fear. Forgiveness frees **us** into the fullness of a life in Christ.

As I adopt a lifestyle of forgiveness and cultivate a forgiving nature (for I believe I can choose to do this) so other aspects of my nature will change and grow. I will find myself seeing others with the compassion of Christ (this might take time), and I can look more kindly on others (this will need practice). But I remember that all things are possible with God, and **I** can do **all things** through Christ who strengthens me. This surely is the key. I press in to Jesus. I seek and ask for His strengthening of me. I receive from Him. Indeed I look to be infilled with the fullness of His presence in me.

John reminds me of my interwoven-ness with Christ. He is the vine and I am a branch of the vine (John 15.5). He chose me. I get excited at this. He appointed me to bear lasting fruit (John 15.6). If I remain in Him and He remains in me, I will bear much fruit. And, indeed, apart from Him I can do nothing (John 15.5). I am aware, right now, that Jesus exhorts me to remain in Him first. His words are:

"If a man remains in me and I in him."

(John 15.5)

This phrase clearly indicates that as **I** remain in **Him**, He will remain in me. The choice is mine. Do I wish to seek Him out to remain in Him? Do I want to follow Him and allow Him to exercise full reign and control in my life? Do I truly mean it when I say "not my will but Yours, not what I want but what you want!" Do I mean all in these things? You bet I do! And why? The answer is simply that I am nothing without Him. He is my all, my reason for living. Without Jesus I have no purpose in life. I might as well be dead, and this is horrific to me, for I don't want to be dead and without Jesus. No, living without Christ is not an option. I will live with Him, for Him and in Him. And with Him living in me.

This is also a state of being. Like so many other mortals I have, for a long time, been fixated with a state of doing. And God has made it so clear to me that He wants me to "be" before I do anything. As "I am" then He will occasion the doing. I can only truly be when I am in Him, and he is fully in me.

Lord, Mighty God,

I come to You in all the fullness of surrender that I can muster. You are everything to me and I lay myself humbly and expectantly at Your feet. I glorify You this day. I rejoice in the sunshine that is without and the revelation that is within.

*And what is this revelation? I think it's the wonder of the true realisation that I am your child. I am Yours! I shout with joy in my total release of myself to You. Take me, my God, and let me **be**, let me truly be – a living, vibrant, true, real, and effective witness for Jesus.*

I am the branch that is grafted firmly into the vine. I seek the life-giving force, the Spirit infilling that comes from the Jesus vine. Feed me, nurture me, and grow me. There may be a price to pay. Make me willing, Lord. In Your holy power change me, and use me if You choose. I ask all these things, believing, in Jesus' name. Amen.

God's house

Then they set out, and the terror of God fell upon the towns all around them so that no one pursued them.

Gen. 35.5

God had spoken to Jacob telling him to go up to Bethel, the place where God had appeared to him previously, and to settle there.

Jacob had named the place Bethel (which means the house of God) because he had experienced an amazing encounter with God in that place. He knew it was a holy place, and a place of divine power.

Whether or not it was this knowledge that moved him we may never know, but in verse 2 we read of Jacob charging his household to rid themselves of all other gods, to purify themselves before the one true God and to dress themselves in clean clothes. This strikes me as somewhat uncharacteristic for the Jacob I have been reading about. Maybe I am a little too cynical. Perhaps Jacob had experienced a true and complete change of heart after his struggles with God. Or maybe his actions were the result of the Holy Spirit's working in him. For whatever reason, I believe he most certainly did the right thing.

And it's as if God endorses this with his blessing. As the clean, purified and God-focused people set out, their mighty God is with them. He protects them from all threat and danger. He leads them safely to the place where He wants them to be. God confirms His promise to Jacob, the promise that comes to him from Abraham and Isaac.

It excites me to read of people being in the place where God wants them to be. In that place they may enjoy the fullness of God's blessing.

God spoke to Jacob and Jacob heard. He responded accordingly after first making sure he was cleansed and prepared for the things of God. He was obedient, and God blessed him.

Lord God,

Thank You for this example and reminder of obedience. I see also in this narration the magnitude of Your power. I ask You to reveal more of this power to me. I pray that I might come to a place of knowledge and active respect for the greatness that is You. May I be blessed to see Your power in action in my life?

I seek a divine harmony between my head and my heart and I ask for Your intervention and working in me so that, daily, I experience more and more of the reality of who You are and what You are able to do. Show me more of Your glory, Your might and Your easy ability to do anything, to change any present circumstance and to bring forth a new thing that will liberate, heal and bring glory to You, O Great God. Amen.

Abounding love

And this is my prayer: that your love may abound more and more in knowledge and depth of insight, so that you may be able to discern what is best and may be pure and blameless until the day of Christ, filled with the fruit of righteousness that comes through Jesus Christ – to the glory and praise of God.

Phil. 1.9-11

Paul is writing to the Philippians but, as so often with God's holy Word, I appropriate his prayer for myself. He is writing this letter, which is sometimes known as the letter of Joy, from the confines of a prison. In this he is clearly reminding us that the physical environment and our material well-being do not dictate the state of spiritual life in us and our experience of joy.

Joy comes from the love of Christ. Firstly, the love that Christ has for us and expresses to us. Then the love that Christ places in us, which bubbles up inside and gives release in joyous and joyful expression. And also there is the love of Christ that flows out from us, releasing His joy through us, touching all we meet with the sweet fragrance of the Saviour in us.

Christ's love is to be experienced. Paul's prayer is that I will receive more of this love that it might abound in me. He prays for an increase of knowledge and insight. I say, "Yes, please." He prays that I might know discernment such that I can choose what is best, and that I may be pure and blameless until our Lord's return. I say, "Yes, please". Paul asks that I be filled with the fruit of righteousness, the righteousness of Jesus Christ which I may express through all of my being to the glory and praise of God. I say, "Yes, please."

Lord God,

I endorse Paul's prayer for myself. I cannot express it with any greater clarity than he does, but I add my own ardour. I want to be filled – to **overflowing** with the fullness of Jesus Christ. I want Him to ooze out of every pore of my being. I want Him to be seen in all that I am and everything that I do. May the fruit of His righteousness ripen and flourish in me.

Holy Father, hear my prayer. I will not be satisfied until I am filled with all the fullness of Christ. Help me in this. I give myself to You Amen.

Pouring out

In bitterness of soul Hannah wept much and prayed to the LORD...

"Not so, my lord," Hannah replied, "I am a woman who is deeply troubled. I have not been drinking wine or beer; I was pouring out my soul to the LORD."

1 Sam. 1.10,15

Hannah was desolate. Though her husband loved her dearly, her womb was closed. She had no children and this saddened her. Her husband's other wife, Peninnah, who had many children, tormented and provoked her. During their annual visit to the temple to worship and sacrifice to the Lord, Hannah would be so upset and distraught that she found herself praying with much bitterness of soul. She was tormented by the lack of children in her life. It was obviously God's will and it caused her so much pain. Consequently she would have spoken out of a mood that might seem hardly conducive to prayer. Indeed Eli the priest thought she was drunk. Her lips moved in prayer, but no sound came from her mouth. Eli told her to be rid of her wine. She replied by telling him of her deep distress. She was troubled. How difficult it must have been for her to hold these things in her heart and yet pray out to the Lord. But this is what she did. She poured out her soul to the Lord. I have a sense that, in her abject misery, she emptied her heart before God, dumping everything, possibly with the bitterest complaint directed to Him.

And the Lord responded in blessing. He heard Hannah's cry. He opened her womb and blessed her with a child, not only a child but a son, most precious in those days. Hannah in her gratefulness, and in obedience to her prior promise, dedicated her son, Samuel, to the service of the Lord. And a mighty man of God ministered and witnessed to the world!

Why did God respond to Hannah's prayer which came out of the bitterness of her heart? Maybe out of love and compassion! I sense that her honesty played a part. She was heartbroken and despairing, and possibly blaming the Lord. And it appears that she said so. God received her honesty, and responded in love.

Dear Lord,

I thank You that we can come to You whatever our state is. Even in the depths of bitterness we are able to cry out to You and to release our pain and anguish to You.

I thank You for the security and safety of being able to bring our deepest concerns and fears to You. But, more than this, I thank You that You respond to us in mercy, grace and love. You hear and You receive our heartaches, and You bring comfort and relief. In Hannah's case You brought the blessing of a son.

Lord God, nothing is impossible for You. Your love saves and releases, empowers and blesses. May I ever live in the safe-keeping of Your love. May I know Your protection and guidance at all times, In Jesus' name I pray. Amen.

Open doors

...These are the words of the holy one, the true one,
who has the key of David,
who opens and no-one will shut,
who shuts and no one opens.

Rev. 3.7b NRSV

The Holy One is the true one, and He is able to do **all** things.

I am reminded of the words I received some time ago when God spoke to me through an intermediary. He said He would open doors for me and He wanted me to walk through whatever doors He opened. He also said He would close doors, and He did not want me to attempt to go through any doors that He would close.

Right now, a lot seems to be happening in my life. There are doors that might be opening. Is God at work? Do I wait to see if He opens wide any of these doors? Do I ask Him to firmly shut any doors that He might not be opening for me?

I have often told people that I do not consider God to be tricky or sneaky. His word exhorts us to ask, to seek and to knock – and we will receive, we will find, and the door will be opened.

Lord God,
I thank You for who You are and I thank You for adopting me as Your precious well-loved child.
I seek to do Your will. I want only to do Your will.
I ask You, Precious Father, to open wide the doors that You would have me go through. And I ask You to close

*absolutely any doors whatsoever, that may be open or opening,
if it is not Your will that I go through them.*

*I love You. I want so much to work for You. Hallelujah!
Praise Your Name. Amen.*

Revive me... again

**Will you not revive us again,
that your people may rejoice in you?
Show us your unfailing love, O LORD,
and grant us your salvation.**

Psalm 85.6,7

Isn't this the truth? The psalmist asks God for revival – **again.**
And the situation is all too typical for each generation and
every age.

We are touched by God, and we respond. We receive His
free and willing offer of salvation. We walk and talk with Him
and life is just wonderful. Then we somehow lose it. Maybe not
completely, but the sparkle fades, the closeness becomes more
distant, and the world and its distractions become more immediate
and, often, more appealing.

This is where I wouldn't blame God if He dumped me. But
He doesn't! Time and again He doesn't give up on me. It's as if He
refuses, like He's saying, *"I will not let you go!"*

When the psalmist calls for a show of God's unfailing love, I
believe he does so knowing that God will respond affirmatively
and warmly. God is ever loving and ever faithful. What an amazing
combination. And how blessed – just how blessed – I am to know
His reviving, His faithfulness and love and the fullness of His
salvation - continually.

Lord God,

I come to You without pretence. I know full well that I do not deserve relationship with You. I know equally that I crave it, and can't get enough. In fact, I'm addicted to You.

I rejoice that my knowing You is not dependent upon my credentials. Please hear me when I say, with sincerity in my heart, that I do not take this lightly, or for granted.

I'm sorry for my sinful state. Please forgive me, and continue to forgive me. Restore me to the joy of salvation and the fullness of relationship with You. Receive my homage and humble adoration, in Jesus' name I ask. Amen.

Living in Love

God is love. Whoever lives in love lives in God, and God in him.

1 John 4.16b

What a beautifully simple statement: God is love. These three words say it all – almost. There is more. Anyone who lives in love lives in God and God in him. This wonderful communion comes from "living" in love. I see this quite differently from "touching" in love, or "passing in and out" of love.

Jesus said clearly, "Love your enemies and pray for those who persecute you." I see this and I understand it, yet it is not easy to do. And if someone who is not even on the fringe of being an enemy says or does something that criticises or upsets me I am immediately defensive and often, in my defence, I attack. This is not love and, as I say, this is not really my enemy. How can I hope to love my enemies when I often struggle to love those who are nowhere near being enemies. I have a long way to travel in "living" in love.

Lord God,

As surely as I see the totality of living in love, I also see my own shortcomings. There is a weakness within me in regard to fully loving. This creates an opportunity for Your strength to touch and fill me and lead me forward, in Your way, to love.

I seek to live in love. I want to impart the presence of Jesus to all I meet in this life. I can do this only in, and through, You.

Dear God of love, please touch me with Your love. Impart to me the love You have for Your children. Let me see them as You see them. Lead me to see where they hurt and to minister to that hurt. Show me, please, the wonderful things that You see in Your children. Help me to help them uncover the true person that God made them to be. But let me do all in love.

I love You. I know You love me. I ask You to lead me forward, in love, spreading and sharing as I go, in Jesus' name. Amen.

Not ruined

"Woe to me!" I cried. "I am ruined! For I am a man of unclean lips, and I live among a people of unclean lips, and my eyes have seen the King, the LORD Almighty."
Isa.6.5

Isaiah cries out with dismay because he has seen the Lord God, and anyone who saw God expected to die immediately. Rather than die, Isaiah was commissioned by God to a prophetic ministry among his people. A seraph touched his lips with a live coal taken from the altar. This act set Isaiah free, atoning for his sin and taking away his guilt.

Today I seem to want to cry, "Woe is me!" but my reasons differ from those of Isaiah. I yearn desperately (yes, I don't see that as too strong a word) to connect with God, to enjoy deep intimacy with Him and to be involved in ministry for Him arising out of the depth of relationship. This is my heart's desire and I know God knows this. But it doesn't seem to be happening – at least not as swiftly as I would like it!

As I write I am reminded, yet again, of Matthew 6.33: ***But seek first his kingdom and his righteousness, and all these things will be given to you as well.***

I **know** this is what I'm meant to do!!

Dear Lord,

*I shall quote from my favourite hymn and also call You "Father of mankind". And the next line – "Forgive our foolish ways". This really, today, needs to be forgive **my** foolish ways.*

I am a silly son! I come before You in humility. I confess to You my lack of total faith. I confess that I do not trust You with the completeness that I need to. I confess the doubt I sometimes feel that I will not enter into the fullness of intimate relationship with You. I confess my lack of faith that You will provide for all of my needs – spiritual, emotional, intellectual, physical and material, and that Your provision will be abundant, I confess anything else that my poor memory might have overlooked but of which You will be fully aware. I confess all these things and earnestly repent of them before You.

I ask You to remove the blinkers from my eyes, take out the plugs from my ears, demolish any shutters that might restrict and confine my thinking, and melt any hardness whatsoever that might be in my heart.

Let me know the sweetness of Your presence. I come near,
Lord, and I wait in excited expectancy. Draw me close; feed
my soul, my heart, my spirit. Have Your way, in Jesus' name
I ask. Amen.

Righteousness

For in the gospel a righteousness from God is revealed,
a righteousness that is by faith from first to last, just as
it is written: "The righteous will live by faith."

Rom 1.17

Paul encapsulates the gospel perfectly in this one verse. The gospel is all about righteousness – being put right with God. It's not about prosperity or the good life now. Those things might happen for some Christians, but unlikely for all.

Righteousness will not come by our doing. The law has failed. It shows us, more than anything else, the power and pestilence of sin. Righteousness is from God. And He – praise His glorious name – chose to restore us to right relationship with Himself by sending His Son to earth to live a sinless life, but to die, vicariously, for our sin. The righteousness of God begins anew for us when we first turn to Christ in repentance and receive salvation. The Holy Spirit leads us on a journey of growing righteousness through this earthly life with the hope of eternal glory to come.

Our part is to receive this wonderful gift by a demonstration of faith. We receive Christ by faith, we live in this present life to the very best we can by the power of the Holy Spirit – through faith. And, in faith we look forward to the glory to come. What a wonderful and truly miraculous combination – the righteousness of Almighty God and my faith – and even that (faith) is God given.

Lord God,

I exalt You. I praise Your rich and wonderful name. I thank You for the gift of faith which has enabled me to come to You and receive the gift of righteousness. I thank You for the amazing gift of Your Holy Spirit. I ask You, by Your Holy Spirit, to guide me in all righteousness in this present life. Convict me when I need to change my ways. Strengthen and encourage me to do so. Lead me forward into eternal glory, in Jesus' name I ask. Amen

Power and protection

The LORD is my strength and my shield; my heart trusts in him, and I am helped.

My heart leaps for joy and I will give thanks to him in song.

Psalm 28.7

The power I need comes from the Lord God. He is my protection. Indeed, He is all I need and want.

I can agree with the psalmist that my heart trusts in Him. I truly believe there is no problem with this. But my head does not always align with the truth of my heart. My head will often, perhaps too often, look at the existing situation and the natural context and environment and be totally influenced by what it sees. My head will discard those two truths that God has been so wanting me to take hold of **with all my being:** Nothing is impossible for God, and I can do all things through Christ who strengthens me.

This is God's reality. The workings of my mind in looking at, and being influenced by, the worldly view of what confronts me are to be shunned, ignored, and replaced by the greater spiritual reality that God is my all. He is my provider and protector; I need nothing else when I am truly in Him.

In this truth my heart leaps for joy. As I live in the glorious reality of who I am in Him, I cannot fail to give Him thanks, loud and long, with my heart and with my voice.

God is my way. He is everything – the morning light, the brightness of the day, and the restfulness of the night. He is peace, peace in all things. In Him I am secure. In Him I am equipped for all that He asks of me, all that He would have me do for Him.

Right now my heart leaps within me. I rejoice with a song of praise and glory. I am filled with hope and expectation. I embrace my Lord God with all of my being, rejoicing in His wonderful Being, and in who I am in Him.

Lord God,

Glorious One, Mighty and Loving Father, Gracious Provider and Protector,

I love You, Lord, my King and my Dad. You truly are everything to me. My heart sings out today in outrageous praise and thanksgiving. Receive all I have to offer. Receive me please, gladly and joyfully. I commit myself wholly, and whole-heartedly, to You. Quite simply, I just want to serve You. And so, I will journey into this day believing for Your guidance, provision and protection. I will embrace what You send and rejoice in what befalls. Hopefully I will honour You and bring true worship in all that I do. Receive this, my humble and sincere prayer, in Jesus' name. Amen.

One Father

And do not call anyone on earth 'father', for you have one Father, and he is in heaven.

Matt. 23.9

These words amaze me because for me they are absolutely true.

I have known no earthly father. There was a time when this was loss to me, a great loss. But that time is long since gone. When, in later life, I joined in new relationship with my heavenly Father, I knew this was my true Father. I rejoice in the sweetness of that relationship which has been so from the first, yet gets deeper and sweeter with each passing day. I am able to rejoice also that there is no earthly father, no inferior example to cloud or confuse me. I have been blessed with a unique father-son relationship. I thank my Father today and I will continue to thank Him for the most wonderful relationship He has drawn me into.

My Dear, Dear Father,

I thank You, truly, for sparing me the imperfections of an earthly father. Yet I bow low before You in the realisation that it was Your plan – since before time began – to bless me with the perfect Father. I am almost speechless. You have taken my breath away, after all this time, after those early, seemingly endless years of deprivation and longing for a dad. Through the hate and anger towards the human who should have been there for me. Then came the joy of meeting You and the years of healing and release. I am growing, still growing, in relationship with You and the marvel of knowing a true Father – absolutely the best Dad of all.

Sweet Daddy, I feel today as if something has been brought to completion. Your Word promises wonderfully that the good work You begin You will carry to completion. A stage has been reached, and I now release myself further and more fully into my relationship with You as a much loved and favoured child of the most wonderful Father.

Holy Dad, receive my thanks, my appreciation, my love – and me. Hallelujah! Amen.

===

Thank offerings

He who sacrifices thank offerings honours me, and he prepares the way so that I may show him the salvation of God.

Psalm 50.23

There is so much to thank God for, yet there are times when I might be so pre-occupied with a presenting problem that I cannot clearly see the things I could be thankful for. Indeed, there are times when my immediate concerns so overwhelm me that I cannot bring myself to be thankful for anything.

This is perhaps where the sacrifice comes in. I am well aware of the exhortation to praise God at all times and in all circumstances, but I am also too painfully aware of how difficult this sometimes is. Then I need to bring forth the sacrifices, declaring the righteousness, the goodness and the love of God in the midst of any negative focus I might have.

Lord God,

I understand that to praise and thank You is a choice. Right now, it is not a difficult choice for me to make. I rejoice in You. I thank You for a new day and a new start for life in me today. I sing Your praises. You are wonderful. I feel Your presence with me and I rejoice.

But there are times when I find it difficult to make the choice to thank and honour You. At these times I need help. Your Word assures me that You are always with me and so I ask You to help me at these times. May Your Holy Spirit lead me into that place where I might rest in You – and be thankful.

No problem I can ever face is too big for You. Hallelujah! You are my Lord and my God. You will lead me through. I will fear nothing as I face it with You.

Holy One, I thank You. I honour You with my prayer and praise. Receive these, and me, in Jesus' name I ask. Amen.

Walk in love

And this is love: that we walk in obedience to his commands. As you have heard from the beginning, his command is that you walk in love.

2 John 6

Again we have the mix of love and command. If we love God we will obey His commands. And His commands are that we love – Him and each other. In this letter John states God's command as to walk in love. This brings a beautiful picture to my mind, a picture of the believer walking everywhere in love – walking with God and walking with all of God's creation in love. I see this applying to all things, all aspects of creation.

Yet it is not easy to walk in love. This is not a mushy, sentimental sloppiness. Rather it is a commitment, and one that requires diligence and perseverance. Walking lovingly with some- one does not mean agreeing with them in everything and tolerating all that they do. Rebuke may well be part of love. Often there are things we are called upon to do which we might choose not to do if we had a choice. I believe, notwithstanding we might be called to do something that is difficult, we can still explore the best way to implement what we must do. If anyone is to be confronted with a painful truth, the process of "walking in love" will yield the way to act that is least painful and most loving. This is not to suggest that the subject matter is to be diluted. It must be clearly presented, but without judgment or condemnation.

Indeed, loving God will involve us in necessary rebuke and correction from Him when this is needed. An interesting part of loving someone is that we don't want them to find anything wrong or unacceptable in us. We want them to delight in us and strongly affirm us. Yet true love will willingly receive rebuke where it is warranted. True love will receive it and be willing to be changed.

And so, love is a give and take arrangement. God is love and He is the place for me to start as I desire to go forward "walking in love".

Dear Lord,

I'm reading, learning and receiving much about love. I thank You for Your impartation. I love you and I rejoice in knowing and experiencing Your love for me.

I desire to walk in love. I yearn to please You in all that I do. I want also to live in the utmost loving relationships with all people. None of this is easy. I will not always please You, and there will be many times when I might struggle to love others and do the right thing by them.

I seek Your help, Lord. I ask You to lead me in a walk of love. My prayer is that it will last for the whole of my life. I invite You to daily show me the way, Your way, and to lead me in it. What a powerful force love is! Let me walk in it, always. In Jesus' name I ask. Amen.

Foundation or fall

The LORD Almighty is the one you are to regard as holy,
he is the one you are to fear,
he is the one you are to dread,
and he will be a sanctuary;
but for both houses of Israel he will be
a stone that causes men to stumble
and a rock that makes them fall.
And for the people of Jerusalem he will be a trap and
a snare.

Isa. 8.13, 14

The Lord is either the solid foundation upon which we fully stand, or He is a rock over which we will fall.

When we commit to Him as our foundation we need to acknowledge and respect certain things about Him. We are to regard Him as holy. How do we interpret holy? Firstly, it is divinely sacred. God is divinely sacred. His holiness is intense. It can sear and burn if we get too close. But, at a respectful distance, treated with reverence and awe, the holiness of God will bless abundantly. The love and grace of God spills out of his holiness. The perfect sanctuary will be found, in holy wonder and awe, in the Lord Almighty.

How great this truth is! I pray that I may never stumble or fall in my Lord God, but ever know Him as a sanctuary, a refuge, a place of rest, refreshing and restoring.

Lord God,

I come to You as my sanctuary. I come in reverential fear and awe. I come to worship You. I come to rest in You. You are my portion. You are my everything. My life is nothing without You.

I pray You will receive my homage and respect. I bow before Your holiness. I worship and honour You. Amen.

Denied... but

But Peter declared, "Even if I have to die with you, I will never disown you." And all the other disciples said the same.

Matt. 26.35

Jesus has told Peter that he will deny Him three times, but Peter protests. As the story unfolds there is not even the smallest hint that Peter will stand by Jesus. Yes, he follows Him into the courtyard of the high priest's home, but his courage fails him. When questioned, he falls to the pattern of denial that Jesus had prophesied.

Peter is often held before us in this example of weakness and "folding". But the truth is that all of the disciples deserted Jesus. He had told them, **"This very night you will all fall away on account of me."** They had all responded as Peter had – **Then all the disciples deserted him and fled.** (v56)

These events serve as a further reminder that no one is worthy of Jesus. We all fall short and, I'm sure, we all disappoint Him greatly at different times. But this did not stop Him in His mission. He came to seek and to save the lost. He entered the world as a baby – innocent and humble. He left the world by the cruel actions of sinful man, but He remained innocent and humble. His humility saw Him live every moment of His earthly life in obedience to the heavenly Father. His innocence fitted Him as the perfect sacrifice to restore sinful man to a righteous God.

Thank God for Jesus. We ourselves are not worthy, but He enables us to enter into renewed relationship with the Almighty.

Lord God,

This day I especially say Thank You.

Thank You for coming to this earth to make the way for me to return to You.

Thank You for receiving me back in relationship.

Thank You for healing me.

Thank You for growing me.

Thank You. Amen.

Who are you, Lord?

He asked, "Who are you, Lord?"

Acts 9.5a NRSV

I find this question to be so exciting, and more than a little enigmatic in regard to the answer it might bring.

It is asked by Paul, as Saul, when he is bombarded by the bright light on the road to Damascus. The answer he receives is:

"I am Jesus, whom you are persecuting."

From what we know of Paul's subsequent relationship with Jesus it is clear that he, in time, received much revelation and insight in response to this question. Paul knew and loved Jesus. I sense that Paul got quite a full answer to his question, "Who are you, Lord?"

I pray I will, over the course of time, receive a full answer. I pray that I might come to know and love Jesus as Paul did.

Lord Jesus,

I want to ask "Who are You?"

I know who You are, but I want to know You more. I desire a closer habitation with You. I seek a deeper relationship *with You. The question, "Who are You, Lord?" excites me. It opens my mind and my heart to all sorts of wonderful revelations of You, to the most amazing insights and sharings with You, and to a life lived completely in Your company. This is what I want, Lord. I want to **know** You and to live in the fullness of life in You. Show me who You are, in Your precious name I ask. Amen.*

J trust...

I trust in the LORD.
I will be glad and rejoice in your love,
for you saw my affliction and knew the anguish of my soul.
You have not handed me over to the enemy
but have set my feet in a spacious place.

Psalm 31.6b-8

Oh, the truth of real relationship with God. How good it is to declare "I trust in the Lord" and know it is not a wild declaration. For some time God has been challenging me to place my full trust in Him. That's right, my **full** trust. I generally have no problem in trusting God but I do sense that, hitherto, it has been something of a general trust. The challenge in recent times has been for a full, total, complete surrender to Him, placing every particle of trust in him and believing – implicitly and explicitly, for His will.

As I look to Him, as I fix my eyes on Jesus, and continue to focus on Him, I need not be concerned at all about what I do. He is all I need and He will lead me into whatever I am to do. This conviction grows in me. With it comes an even stronger desire to look to Him and to keep focused on Him. I am able to spend every second in His company, and this assuredly keeps me well and truly anchored in His will. I trust in the Lord. How joyfully I am able to express this sentiment today. I see Him. I receive his love. I am glad, and I rejoice in the wonder of my relationship with Him.

Lord God,

I thank You for Your eternal presence with me. I invite You into all that I am. I ask You to lead me in all that I do. I trust You. I marvel at Your power, Your glory and Your presence manifest to me and alive and real in me through Your Holy Spirit. I rejoice in Your faithfulness. You know all about me. You know and yet You love me. I embrace the wonder of Your love. I marvel at the endless expressions of Your love that I see in this life. Yet there is room for more.

I open myself to You and ask that the fullness of Your will be outworked in my life. May I know even more of Your love, but may I be used by you to share and spread Your love in every place that I visit and every experience I encounter.

I trust You and surrender fully to Your love and Your will. Receive my love and adoration, in Jesus' name I pray. Amen.

Hid in Jesus

Therefore, brothers, since we have confidence to enter the Most Holy Place by the blood of Jesus...

Heb 10.19

Jesus died once and for all time, and His blood – and only His blood – opened the way for us to enter in. I cannot enter the Most Holy Place by my own endeavours. I can only do so because Jesus offered Himself in atonement for my sin.

I have this amazing mental picture of a sinful me. I cannot stand before our righteous God because His total purity will not tolerate any impurity. Yet in the picture I see myself facing God and receiving the richness of His blessings and the fullness of life in Him. This is possible because in my picture Jesus stands in the gap between me and God, and all my impurity is filtered and removed by His purity.

I see a trinity in this picture. Jesus is in the Father, and I am in Jesus and He is in me (John 14.20).

Lord Jesus,

I lift Your name with the mightiest HALLELUJAH I can express. Thank You, O thank You for Your sacrifice for me, making possible my return to the Father, Thank You, Lord. Thank You, Sweet Jesus. Amen.

Secret thoughts

...and their conflicting thoughts will accuse or perhaps excuse them on the day when, according to my gospel, God, through Jesus Christ, will judge the secret thoughts of all.

Rom. 2.15b, 16 NRSV

I don't think my thoughts are always pleasing to God.

I am aware of Paul's encouragement to the Corinthians: ***"...we take every thought captive to obey Christ"*** (2 Cor. 10.5). I try to do this, yet I often fall short.

I turn again, of course, to God whose Word tells me to ask. Indeed, His Word **assures** me that if I ask I shall receive. He means me to ask for those things that are right in Him. I feel sure it would be right in Him for me to think always thoughts that are in full obedience to Christ.

Lord God,

You know that my thoughts are not always in obedience to Christ. I repent and ask Your forgiveness. I desire to set aside all thoughts that are not in accordance with Your will, and that might be displeasing to You. I do not want this so. I am unable to overcome in my own strength. I need You, Lord. I ask for Your help and power to overcome. Please lead me, Lord, and enable me to take every thought captive in true and full obedience to my Lord Jesus Christ. Hear me, and help me, in Jesus' name I ask. Amen.

His will

Teach me to do your will,
for you are my God;
may your good Spirit
lead me on level ground.

Psalm 143.10

These words of the psalmist are most encouraging. I might struggle within myself; even strive to seek out God's will for me. I might anguish, daily, to be sure that I am living in His will. Yet none of this is necessary. For, just like the psalmist, all I need do is to surrender myself to the Almighty and say, simply:

Lord, teach me to do Your will. You are my God. You are almighty and I choose to live in Your will. You will teach me and I rejoice in this.

I am grateful to have come to the place of trusting God for His will, and believing that I live in it from moment to moment. I repeatedly tell Him that my desire is to live in the fullness of His will. Having done this, and continuing to do it, I believe that God's will is not some future event that I must await, but that it's with me right at this moment. For, as surely as I've asked, He has responded and I live in His will in the here and now.

The psalmist further asks for God's Spirit to lead him on level ground. Again, I want always to be led by the Holy Spirit. It would be most desirable if life were lived at all times "on level ground", but sometimes the journey takes us into mountainous terrain. We travel through valleys; we are challenged by dark shadows and steep ascents. Yes, it would be nice if the journey was always on level ground but this does not always happen. Yet, with the Holy Spirit as our travel companion, we need not fear the undulations of life. Living in God's will, I know that God is always there. Indeed, His Word assures me of this. And ultimately, despite what might arise along the way, God will come through. He will have His way and the result will be peace and blessing. Level ground is desirable but not necessary to my walk of faith with a righteous and faithful God.

Lord God,

How wonderful it is to echo a voice of long ago and say, in unison with this ancient writer: teach me to do Your will. You know how I long to please You, how I desire to live in the fullness of Your will – right now and for every moment of life. I rejoice because I have brought this plea before You many times, and I believe You have heard and answered. I choose to believe that I live in Your will right now and for every minute that I continue to keep my eyes fixed on You.

I seek the constant leading of Your Spirit. I do not wish to go anywhere or do anything without your Holy Spirit leading me. Let me be led by the Spirit as my Lord Jesus was led in all that He did on this earth. Lord, hear my prayer.

May I also live a Godly life, pleasing to You in every respect and fulfilling the specific plan and purposes You have for me. I come to You in love and obedience. I'm Yours. Hallelujah! Amen.

In Spirit and peace

And with that he breathed on them and said, "Receive the Holy Spirit."

John 20.22

Jesus is commissioning the disciples for their work of spreading the gospel. He has just said to them, **"Peace be with you! As the Father has sent me, I am sending you."**

They go out in peace, the hallmark of Jesus, and the sign in all Christians of Christ in them.

They are sent. Jesus was sent by the Father to fulfil a specific mission. The disciples were sent by Jesus and their mission was specific – to preach the gospel and to make disciples.

They are filled with the Holy Spirit. This gentle presence is God's power in us and with us. God works through us by His Holy Spirit. The miraculous power of God is manifest on earth today through the person of the Holy Spirit. He often will work in and through true disciples.

Jesus further exhorted those first disciples: **"If you forgive anyone his sins, they are forgiven; if you do not forgive them, they are not forgiven."** Forgiveness of sins is a mark of the true Christian. The believer (new and mature) demonstrates the degree of their faith by the ability to forgive. In asking for forgiveness we demonstrate repentance.

The disciple is a "sent one", sent out by the Lord Jesus to minister the gospel of salvation. He or she goes out in peace, symbolic of the presence of the Saviour. They are empowered by the Holy Spirit to bring the lost into new life in Jesus, to grow them as disciples, and to lead them into a lifestyle of repentance and forgiveness.

Those early disciples were the first. Down through the centuries Jesus has been commissioning faithful servants and sending them out to spread the gospel. The work continues today. Each one who comes to Christ is called. In some way we are all sent out to do the work that the Master has allocated for us. May we go in peace. May we be filled with the Holy Spirit and know His power in us as we share the gospel of faith, as we teach of the love and sacrifice of Jesus, and the way to live in Him in repentance and forgiveness.

Lord God,

I thank You for those early disciples who were obedient to the word of the Master. I thank You for the disciples through the ages who have passed on the good news and kept the flame of faith alight and burning. I thank You for today's disciples who have greater numbers of unsaved to be reached than at any other time. The time is precious and the message must be spread. I pray for the commissioning of each and every one who calls themselves Christian. For, I believe, all who come to Christ have a mission to spread the good news, to preach the gospel and to make disciples.

I pray an anointing of peace on each and every one of your chosen ministers. Let them know the peace of Jesus. Take them out to minister in His peace and to transmit His peace into this stressful world. In Jesus' name I ask. Amen.

Known by God

But the man who loves God is known by God.

1 Cor. 8.3

Paul has been talking about knowledge. He informs us that knowledge puffs up, but love builds up. Love is needed together with knowledge. As I temper my knowledge with love toward God, I can be assured that I am truly known by God and accepted as one of His redeemed.

Of course my love for God will lead me into love for others. Love comes from God; God is love. And the love of God will fill me to the point where I must share it.

I rejoice in this. To know God, truly, is to love Him. To love God is to be known by Him. To love Him is to be led to love others – the poor, the lost, and the homeless - to love them, and to show them the way to the Father from whom all love comes. And so to Jesus, who is the way, the only way. Come, Lord Jesus, come.

Lord God,

I love You. I rejoice that I am known by You. I seek, always, greater knowledge of You and a greater awareness of the love You have for me.

I want to share Your love. I ask You to strengthen me so that I may be equipped by You for the task. Lead me, please, into God-appointed encounters. Give me the words to speak forth and the actions to live out, in love.

Hear my prayer. Receive it. Answer it, in Jesus' name I ask. Amen.

Consuming fire

When Moses went up on the mountain, the cloud covered it, and the glory of the LORD settled on Mount Sinai. For six days the cloud covered the mountain, and on the seventh day the LORD called to Moses from within the cloud. To the Israelites the glory of the LORD looked like a consuming fire on top of the mountain. Then Moses entered the cloud as he went on up the mountain. And he stayed on the mountain forty days and forty nights.

Exod. 24.15-18

What does this passage tell me? As I imagine the cloud covering the mountain with the glory of the Lord within it, my heart leaps inside me. I feel envy toward Moses, but also a strong sense of awe at the immediacy and power of the presence of God. Moses is, presumably, adjacent to and quite near this cloud of power and glory. He remains in the vicinity for six days. Then, on the seventh day, God calls to him from within the cloud. I almost physically jump at the imagining of the voice of God calling out to Moses.

The Israelites, looking on from afar, are not un-affected. They see the glory of the Lord sitting like a consuming fire on top of the mountain.

Moses enters the cloud. Surely he is touched, impacted and changed by the glory of the Lord. He is with the Lord, in close relationship, for forty days and forty nights. How thrilling, how frightening, terrifying and – how wonderful!

Lord God,
Touch me with Your consuming fire. Draw me into the cloud of Your presence. Let me experience something of Your glory. I know I may not bear all that You could show, but

*I ask for a touch, that I might know the presence and the
awesome power of the living God. My prayer today is indeed
short, that I might meet with You and see something of Your
glory. Thank You, Lord. Amen.*

Faith exercised

*...because she thought, "If I just touch his clothes, I will
be healed." Immediately her bleeding stopped and she
felt in her body that she was freed from her suffering.*

*At once Jesus realised that power had gone out from him.
...*

*He said to her, "Daughter, your faith has healed you.
Go in peace and be freed from your suffering."*

Mark 5.28-30a, 34

Wow, the power of knowing Jesus as Lord and Saviour!

The woman who was subject to bleeding had suffered for twelve years. She had exhausted worldly resources in her search for healing. But she readily recognised the power of life in Jesus. She had faith. She also knew that her faith needed to be exercised. Knowing, believing, that Jesus would heal her was not enough. She needed to touch Him. And when she did, the power of God healed her instantly. Jesus knew that power had gone from Him.

I firmly believe that we will receive power as we press in to Jesus. As we touch Him, He releases power, healing power, into us and through us. This is a definite and deliberate act by Him. He knows that power is coming to us from Him. He wants power to come to us from Him. This is further confirmed by Mark (6.56) as Jesus and the disciples ministered in the region of Galilee – *and all who touched him were healed.*

There is more! The woman who touched Jesus knew she had been healed – she had received divine power. Jesus knew that power had gone out of Him. But there was more action to come. Jesus went on to affirm the healing and empowering. I see this as a significant act. I rejoice in Jesus' affirmation. The woman pressed in to Him without openly showing Him. This could almost be seen as a furtive act. But it is not so. Jesus willingly released power and healing. Similarly there may be times when we feel unworthy, and too unclean to come to Him. I believe the act of our coming is sufficient. Simply in turning to Him, we declare His Lordship in our lives, and our desire to be filled and led by him.

So, what have I learned from today's reflection:

1. Faith is the basis of LIFE – and I only need faith as big as a mustard seed for starters.
2. Faith needs action, and the best possible action for me is to press in to Jesus, to seek Him in everything.
3. As I press in to Jesus, as I seek to touch Him, I will receive power and this power will heal but will also enable me to go forth in Him and for Him – to achieve His plan and purpose for me.
4. Jesus willingly gives us of His power.
5. Jesus affirms us in healing and power.
6. We can come to Him **whatever** the circumstances. In fact, when circumstances seem most against us (like, after twelve years of bleeding), it is vital that we turn to Him, that we touch Jesus.

Lord Jesus,

You are everything. You have clearly told us You are the Life. You have told us You are the Way, You are the Truth. You are all of this. You are everything. I rejoice in You, precious Saviour. I thank You that I have faith. I thank You for I know that this faith comes to me from You. I ask for greater faith. Lord, increase my faith!

I press in to receive more power from You. You have said I will receive power when the Holy Spirit comes on me and I will be Your witness. Oh, yes Lord! Please may I witness more for You? Let me become a greater witness, a more effective witness.

Lord, may Your power be seen more and more in this needy world. I cry out for lost souls who need You. They need You, Lord, yet they are unaware of it. I pray for a mighty release of Your power — worldwide. I look for it here in Australia, and in all places beyond. Let it flow, Lord. Release it. Set the captives free. Build up the Kingdom of heaven in this place, in Your precious name I ask. Amen.

Praying and asking

For this reason, since the day we heard about you, we have not stopped praying for you and asking God to fill you with the knowledge of his will through all spiritual wisdom and understanding.

Col. 1.9

Paul prayed for the Colossians. I dare to pray for me. I yearn to be filled to overflowing with the knowledge of God's will. I long to live in all spiritual wisdom and understanding. I desire to do only the will of God, to walk so closely to Him that I might be known, like Moses, as His friend or, as David, a man after God's own heart.

The "heartbeat" of God must be wondrous to sense and feel. I pray that my God will draw me close, that He will touch me and change me that I might feel His "heartbeat" and move forward in His will.

Lord God,

Paul prayed for the Colossians, but I pray for myself. I echo Paul's prayer. I ask You to fill me with the knowledge of Your will through all spiritual wisdom and understanding. I yield myself to You. I surrender and ask that You take control.

My prayer is that I may constantly, and continually, meet with You and walk closer with You. I ask You to change me to be more in touch with You, to know a deeper intimacy.

Hear me, my dear Lord. Draw me to You. Reveal Yourself to me. May I know You as Moses and David knew You? May I be used by You as they were? May I serve You for all of my life?

I thank You for the many wondrous things You bring forth in my life. I rejoice in Your grace and mercy, Your strength and empowering.

Take me, please. Enjoy me greatly. Use me mightily, in Jesus' name I ask. Amen.

Standing Firm

By standing firm you will gain life.

Luke 21.19

Jesus spoke to His disciples at length about the signs of the end of the Age. He outlined for them some of the desolate, destructive and de-humanising activities that might be expected. Then He gave this encouragement to stand firm, and He outlined the "prize" such action would gain.

I believe He is here talking about perseverance, standing our ground, persisting, and resisting the onslaughts – not only of the devil and of the world, and also of our own human, sinful nature.

Am I willing to construct a soul in accordance with the new life God has put in me? Can I be strong enough to identify any moods I might experience as my responsibility, arising from my own undisciplined nature? Will I take hold of myself and shake – until any undesirable mood or human frailty is dispensed? Will I do all I can do to release myself to God for Him to do His work in me?

Holy Father, Mighty God,

I realise that I have work to do in myself as well as allowing You to work in me. I pray for the wisdom to identify those things that I need to do; I pray for the courage to do them; and I pray for the willingness to release myself to You and allow You to do what You will in me.

I pray also for the global state, and especially for those believers who may face trial and persecution in these present times. Be with them please Lord. Strengthen them to endure with grace and the knowledge that You are with them, and that You are for them.

Help me; help us all, Lord, in Jesus' name I ask. Amen.

The New Creation

For I am about to create new heavens and a new earth; the former things shall not be remembered or come to mind.

Isa 65.17 NRSV

These words of promise surely brought great hope and excitement to the Israelites. They had seen their country overrun and their beloved Jerusalem desecrated. They had known bondage, suffering and humiliation for so long it is highly likely that thoughts of a better life would be most difficult, if not impossible, for them to entertain.

Yet here is their mighty and fearful God making a promise of newness. It is a promise of love and not punishment, of deliverance from all that has been into something new and wonderful. The people are exhorted to *be glad and rejoice forever in what I am creating* (v18). Such will be the change that the former things – of suffering, deprivation, bondage – shall not be remembered or come to mind. They will simply be forgotten. This, the promise for the people of God is, perhaps, one of the most profound statements of the Old Testament Scriptures.

If we then turn to the New Testament we find in the words of Paul a parallel to this promise. But this new declaration is spoken of the individual and it is not future promise but present reality: *So if anyone is in Christ, there is a new creation: everything old had passed away; see, everything has become new.* (2 Cor 5.17).

Jesus brings us into a state of newness, now! And we are called to live in that new state. As I read in Isaiah the words, *the former things shall not be remembered or come to mind,* I am immediately mindful of the words in Paul, *everything old has passed away.* When we come to Jesus He re-creates us afresh in Him. All of the old, unpleasant features of our lives are extinguished in our new life in Him. But sometimes we tend to not readily let go of *the former things.* To do this may require application on our part. Jesus can, and will, set us free – if we will allow Him. The journey may not be easy, but God is gracious and provides help for us at every stage. Our part is to be willing and courageous, sometimes very courageous. As new creations we sometimes need to "recondition" ourselves, our thinking and behaviour, to the state of newness into which He invites us. In Jesus the old can pass away, the former things need not be remembered nor come to mind.

How wonderful is our God! How great is the love that transforms out of misery to joy!

Holy Father,

I thank You for the words of promise in Isaiah that become reality in Jesus. I receive the newness of creation that He offers. Please help me to lay down all past hurt or bitterness, to leave it behind in the knowledge that it can have no ongoing effect on the new me in Christ.

Empower me by Your Holy Spirit to receive the fullness of Your release and healing, such that the former things shall not be remembered or come to mind. I ask these things of You in the loving and powerful name of my Saviour and Your dear Son, the Lord Jesus Christ. Amen.

Salvation

And they cried out in a loud voice:
"Salvation belongs to our God,
who sits on the throne,
and to the Lamb."

Rev. 7.10

Salvation is a gift and it is a gift from God. Jesus said, **"No one can come to me unless the Father who sent me draws him."** (John 6.44)

Many millions worldwide have not yet come into salvation. Closer to home there are many I know that I would like to see in the body of Christ, in the Kingdom of Heaven.

I may pray for these people I care so much about. I may even share with them, to the extent that they will receive, my love and delight for God. But I cannot bring them into salvation. God alone does that. I trust that my prayers move Him. As the multitude cried out in the revelation that John received so I cry out to our great and wonderful God.

Dear Lord,

*I also cry out **Salvation belongs to our God**. I remember still the wonderful gift You gave me when You drew me to Jesus and brought me into the Kingdom.*

I pray now for family members. I pray for my dear neighbours. I pray for friends and acquaintances. My prayer for each and every one of them is for salvation. Lord God, would You draw them to Jesus? Please open hearts and minds, unblock ears and remove the blinkers from eyes. Let them see You, hear the message of salvation, feel the amazing love, and respond in positive affirmation. I restate Your wish, Lord, that no one shall perish (2 Peter 3.9). This is my desire also.

Please hear my prayer. I commit each and every one of these I pray for to You in humble request for their salvation. I ask this in Jesus' name. Amen.

Getting it right

Now this man Micah had a shrine, and he made an ephod and some idols and installed one of his sons as his priest. In those days Israel had no king; everyone did as he saw fit.

Judges 17.5,6

Micah had stolen quite a substantial amount of silver from his mother. So, at the outset, we see a dubious side to his character. When he hears his mother utter a curse in respect to the theft, he confesses, doubtless fearing the curse and its possible effect. In her gratitude for the return of the silver, his mother consecrates it to the Lord, intending thereby to counteract the curse. At his mother's suggestion, Micah creates a carved image and a cast idol, and sets up a shrine, installing one of his sons as a priest. What they are doing is paganising the worship of the true God. They are in direct contravention of the law:

> *You shall not make for yourself an idol in the form of anything in heaven above or on the earth beneath or in the waters below*
>
> (Exod. 20.4).

Micah is further aided in this paganising behaviour by a Levite claiming descent from Moses, whom he took into his home as a priest (Judges 17.9, 10).

As I reflect on this reading, I sense God give me a caution, and almost a plea. It is as if He's saying:

> *"Micah was not alone in his wandering from the truth. Many others in his time professed to follow me yet strayed from right behaviour in relating to me. This did not cease, not even with the coming of my Son in human form. Still today, in the twenty-first century people follow their own ideas of how they will worship me and, supposedly, follow my will. In the story of Micah you read that Israel had no king and everyone did as he pleased. This is no excuse. I do not accept that you need a "king" or any other leader to keep you legitimate in my presence. Before me, every person is responsible for their own behaviour, and answerable to me, and to me alone.*
>
> *I urge you not to be tempted to follow any fancies of your own thinking. I direct you to the instruction of my Word, and I ask you to give yourself to it. Fix*

your eyes on Jesus. Look to Him in all things. Take up His invitation to "Come, follow me". Be as He would be. Hold close and true to His commandments to love the Lord your God with every part of your being, and to love your neighbour as you would want to be loved yourself. Consider also these words from the older testament to not lean on your own understanding but to trust me with all your heart, and acknowledge me in all things. I will lead you. I will not let you down nor abandon you. I have plans for you and I want to see you realise the plans and purposes that is my will for you. You need nothing else – no rites or rituals, no images or other creations. Keep it simple. Give yourself to me and be willing for me to lead and guide you. And, remember, I love you more than you could possible imagine."

Lord, Mighty God, Precious Saviour and Loving Father,

I come to You in new commitment. I'm not aware of having created any idols or of adopting any divergent practices, but this does not clear me of having done so. If I have, unknowingly or unwittingly, followed such ways, I ask Your forgiveness.

I give myself to You and the ways of Jesus. I desire to focus so intently upon You that I become more and more infused by You. May You fill me and seep out from every pore of my being. Lead me, please, further into You, in Jesus' name I pray. Amen.

The Divine Nature

Through these he has given us his very great and precious promises, so that through them you may participate in the divine nature and escape the corruption in the world caused by evil desires.

2 Peter 1.4

Through God's excellence He has given us great and precious promises. The Holy Scriptures are filled with promises from God. I constantly come across the most wonderful undertakings from Him to me. They excite and greatly encourage me. Each time I say, "There's another one. Lord I claim this promise for myself."

We must receive His promises and live in them and with them. This may require us to adopt habits conducive to promise-living. This is a life of plenty, not want. This is a life of great expectation and of receiving. This is a totally God-centred life, one that looks to Him in all things. This is a life that places Him centrally in everything.

This may not accord with the ways of the world. This is the way of God, and we are called to be obedient and receive.

Lord God,

I love You and I thank You that You are in my life. I give You the place of honour. I acknowledge You at the centre of my life. I look to You in all things. I look to see You in daily living, in every event and happening.

I rejoice in You. Words cannot express the joy and appreciation I have in living in You.

Thank You, O thank You, Precious Lord, Loving Saviour. I receive each and every promise You have for me. Amen.

My portion

My flesh and my heart may fail,
but God is the strength of my heart
and my portion forever.

Psalm 73.26

Through occasional aches and pains I am reminded of my mortal vulnerability. I am getting older and, perhaps, more prone to failure of flesh and heart. But this is not peculiar to me. Every living soul on this earth is aging by the minute, even new born babes. Besides, age is not the singular cause of health problems. The flesh and the heart may experience failure at any age. Consequently, the message I take here for myself can be shared with everyone, for all qualify to receive it.

God is all I need. He is my strength and my shield. My heart is His. He will strengthen it, and me, for as long as He needs to. God is my portion, not just for this moment or day, but for all time. I rejoice, gladly and wildly, that I am in Him. He, truly, will provide all I need and He will guide me, for as long as I will allow Him, in the paths He has chosen for me.

I am not fearful of dying. I know not when it will come. When it does I shall be saddened to leave loved ones behind, but I will rejoice to be received in fullness into my portion – forever.

Lord God,
I rejoice in You. I open myself fully to Your strengthening and Your provisions for me. I surrender to You my flesh and my heart. I pray that I might diligently steward them under Your guidance.

You are all I need. I cry out to You in praise and thanksgiving. You are my shield and strength. My cover is in You. My being comes from You. Lead me on, Lord. Let us continue this journey of life together. I thank You for choosing me. I yield completely to You. Hallelujah! I praise Your Name. Amen.

The way

Lord Jesus,

I have just read through the amazing third chapter of the letter to the Ephesians.

I am reminded that You are the way:

In him and through faith in him we may approach God with freedom and confidence. (v.12)

I hear again Your call to Peter to watch with You for one hour (Matt. 26.40).

Lord, here I am to watch with You. Speak to me. Let me see those things that are revealed as we watch together.

Paul asks the Father to strengthen me, out of His glorious riches, with the Holy Spirit in my inner being that You, my Christ, may dwell in my heart through faith. I have faith, yet I ask for more. I seek more of this glorious gift of God. Lord Jesus, You have seen the "glorious riches". May You share some insight of this with me? I imagine the Father's riches. I see seas shimmering as if filled to abundance with the most precious gems. I see health and vitality abounding. I see, not merely a lack of want, but a bountiful provision. Yet it is neither extreme nor wasteful. And perhaps the "most glorious" of the riches that I see are the saints of God. Their eternal lives shine more gloriously than any of the brightest riches of the Kingdom.

In each shining face I see the fullness of the love of Christ, and the fullness of God.

Paul prays for me to be rooted in this love. The plants that are rooted in the soil of my garden receive all they need for life out of that very soil. Their lives reflect the degree of goodness they have received from the soil. So may it be with me, rooted and established in God's love.

Lord Jesus, reveal to me the width and length, height and depth of Your love. Take me into it. Immerse me fully in Your love such that I live it and breathe it and have my whole being in it (Acts 17.28). Fill me, My Precious Lord, to the measure of all the fullness of God. You are able to do immeasurably more that all I could ask of imagine. I surrender to You in totality. I give myself unreservedly to You. Take me, Lord, and have Your way in me. I love You. Oh, how I love You! Amen

Suffering

For he has graciously granted you the privilege not only of believing in Christ, but of suffering for him as well.
Phil. 1.29 NRSV

I have long seen how faith, the belief in Jesus, stems from God's grace. The Father draws us into relationship with the Son. He woos us as a bridegroom chases his beloved. God's grace abounds in His act of love in taking us into Himself.

I have not, however, seriously contemplated the aspect of suffering being "granted to us" by God's grace. This is quite a statement, and worthy of deep reflection.

God grants us suffering! How peculiar is this, almost contradictory to the concept of God's love. It's almost like saying God loves us so much that He gives us suffering. Yet how preposterous might this really be? Jesus suffered, mightily. The apostles suffered and, throughout the history of the church, faithful men and women of God have suffered.

Jesus said, *"Come, follow me."* When we hear this we might be excused for thinking He's saying, "Come, follow me into glory." Perhaps that is our ultimate destination, but as Paul reminds us elsewhere in his writings, *"...we suffer with him <u>so that</u> we may also be glorified with him"* (Rom 8.17).

In our suffering we are actually sharing with Christ and with all those other faithfuls who have travelled this road. And our suffering, an **honour** granted to us by God, leads us into a richer knowledge of Him and a deeper relationship with Him.

Suffering is not simply "granted" to us by God; it is "graciously granted". This tells me that our suffering is cloaked in God's grace. Again, I am mindful of what Paul says in other parts of his writings:

"...God is faithful, and he will not let you be tested beyond your strength, but with the testing he will also provide the way out so that you may be able to endure it"
(1 Cor 10.13).

And, again

"My grace is sufficient for you, for power is made perfect in weakness"
(2 Cor 12.9).

Where is the grace in suffering? I suggest grace abounds in suffering if we look for it and are willing to acknowledge it. Suffering connects us with Christ and with all the precious saints who have suffered in His name. Suffering leads us to a richer knowledge of Him. Suffering allows God's power to be made supremely manifest in our weakness. Suffering gives us opportunity to demonstrate that God's grace is all we need. In suffering, God draws us closer to Himself and takes us into deeper relationship.

I have seen the effects of suffering in different individuals. The body is ravaged and the mind is often tormented. But I have also seen the strength that the love of, and for, God has manifested in the spirit. The life is gone only when the spirit has departed the body. And whilst that spirit is strong and healthy, life prospers despite whatever suffering may occur.

I don't wish to put my hand up for suffering. But in all that I suffer, and to whatever extent it comes upon me, I pray that I will know the working of God's grace throughout my being and circumstances. I look to know the peace of Jesus, and I ask for my spirit to be so intertwined with God's Holy Spirit that my life will be filled with Him. It will be strong and healthy, and a rich witness to the power of His love.

Nothing lasts for ever in this life. Eventually even suffering will cease, ultimately in the precious release we have into the glorious life to come. Yes, we **will** share in His glory, and if we are called to share in His suffering, may we do so with humility and patience, and with a recognition of God's grace active at all times.

Holy God,

I have learned from this reflection. I would not previously have connected suffering with the gracious action of Your granting. I have now begun to see it differently. And previous experiences with some precious saints whom I have seen endure suffering attest to Your grace at work.

I ask You for further insight. Suffering is, perhaps, an extreme of the human experience. You are showing me clearly that You are there, that we can embrace You firmly in the midst of suffering.

Similarly You are there for me in all of life's experiences. There is nothing that I cannot share with You. This is no new revelation, but it is a welcome reminder.

And so, I open myself further to Your holy input. Be with me, Lord, in all things. Whether I am suffering or if I am experiencing the happiest of times, let me know Your presence with me. I am privileged to journey with You. I thank You for this, and invite You to lead me on, through the day ahead and beyond.

I ask all this in Jesus' precious name. Amen.

My Dad

When I thought, "My foot is slipping," your steadfast love, O LORD, held me up.

Psalm 94.18 NRSV

There are times when I feel quite uncertain. Then, when I turn to God, I am upheld and my way becomes sure. There are times when I can literally feel myself going, and again God comes in with His amazing support and guidance. At other times I sense, "It's too late, I've really done it this time. Here comes the crash!" Yet again, God is there for me. In such instances I might need to deal with pride. Yes, I likely need to swallow a great deal of pride! But God is there, and will come to the rescue if I will allow.

I am but one, and may see my concerns as relatively insignificant in worldly terms. I have heard, and read, of others whose plight is far more perilous that mine, sometimes even deadly. But God upholds them. Indeed, the greater the adversity, the stronger is the testimony – of God's protection, deliverance and blessing.

This is His steadfast love, and it is active. God does not hold back. There are certainly times when I need to come to Him in humble petition. I need to take deep into my being the truth and realisation that nothing, but NOTHING keeps God's love from me. This is basic and vital information. When I feel shame, guilt or unworthiness, particularly if it's connected with actions or thoughts I feel responsible for, the clear action for me is to run to the Father and confess. Satan will delight to attempt to hold me back and persuade me I'm a lost cause, but God's love is greater, and it beckons me back into sweet relationship with Him.

Dear Father,

I read of You holding me up when my foot is slipping and I see a wonderful picture of a dad and his son. And this is what I cherish. I give myself to You for the fullness of this relationship.

Yes, You are God Almighty, but You are also my loving, heavenly Dad. I worship You as Almighty God, and I love You as my Divine Dad.

Can I embrace these two very different aspects of You? I think so! And I marvel at how wonderful, gracious and loving You are. I thank You, in Jesus' name. Amen.

Extreme

Those who went ahead and those who followed shouted, "Hosanna!"
"Blessed is he who comes in the name of the Lord!"
Mark 11.9

Jesus enters Jerusalem in triumph. The crowds clamour for Him, throwing tributes at His feet. Yet, before the week has ended, this same crowd will be shouting, "Crucify him! Crucify him!"

This extreme illustration brings to my mind those today who joyfully receive Jesus as Saviour but, somehow, fail when it comes to making Him Lord of their lives. In time they fall away and it is as if they had not come to Him at all. Indeed, one is tempted to question if they ever knew Him. In a way they crucify Him.

My prayer today is for these people, for their lost salvation and for the hope of reconciliation. I pray also for those who haven't yet come into any sort of relationship with Jesus. May God's Holy Spirit work powerfully all over this world, seeking and saving the lost.

Lord God,

I rejoice that I know You, that I have firmly embraced You as Saviour and Lord.

I pray for those who, at some point, have made a decision for You but then slipped away. I ask for forgiveness for them. I pray for God-sent opportunities for them to be re-united with You in Spirit and in truth. I pray You will minister to them and draw them back to You.

I ask also for those who have never shown any interest in You. Touch them, Lord. I pray for powerful God- encounters for them. Let them see the reality of Your love. Move upon them such that they accept Jesus and move forward in discipleship.

I offer myself to be used by You. My desire is for this to be done in Your way and not with any measure of my will in it.Have Your way in me, Lord. Show me Your way and guide me in it, in Jesus' name I ask. Amen.

Life

…but wherever you go I will let you escape with your life.

Jer. 45.5b

God's greatest gift to me on this earth is my life. And my life on earth will lead me into eternal life with Him. Yet while I live here I can live in Him. The greatest life I can embrace is a life "hid with Christ in God". Am I willing to let God take me into union with Himself? Am I prepared to abandon entirely and let go? Immediately I abandon, I think no more about what God is going to do. I refrain from asking questions. I trust God.

Lord God,

I feel somewhat foolish at the way in which I hold on to things that do not really matter when I put You first. I have said my desire is 'to seek first the kingdom of God', but I believe I'm still coming to understand this in all its true meaning. Lord, I abandon myself to You. I surrender to Your divine sovereignty in my life. I look for You in all things. I look to You in all things. Precious Lord, I praise Your name. Amen.

Clean

While Jesus was in one of the towns, a man came along who was covered with leprosy. When he saw Jesus, he fell with his face to the ground and begged him, "Lord, if you are willing, you can make me clean."

Luke 5.12

The final words in this verse have great impact for me. Jesus can make me clean. Jesus can cleanse the dirtiest, foulest sinner. It is interesting to note that the man who came to Jesus was **covered with leprosy**. This tells me that he was in the advanced rather than preliminary stages of the disease. Jesus' response speaks loudly and lastingly: **"I am willing," he said. "Be clean!" And immediately the leprosy left him.** (v13)

And so it is with the sinful. The person who is enmeshed in the deepest sin can be set free by Jesus. Nothing, but nothing, is too great for Jesus to bring deliverance from. I rejoice in this wonderful truth.

> *Lord Jesus,*
>
> *I rejoice in the health and freedom that is in You. You healed the leper and made him clean. You take the most abject sinner and release them from their sins and bring wholeness and health into their beings. I thank You for this.*
>
> *I release to You those dear to me who need to know relationship with You. I ask You to draw them to You, release them from uncleanness and lead them into wholeness. I extend my plea to all who need the release that the leper experienced. I appeal to your willingness. I thank You. Amen.*

Heart and mind

Set your minds on things above, not on earthly things.
Col. 3.2

Paul reminds his first readers, and us, that we have been raised with Christ. In another place he declares that anyone in Christ is a new creation – **the old has gone, the new has come!** (2 Cor. 5.17) We, therefore, need to discard the old and live with, and in, the new.

In verse 1 of this chapter Paul exhorts us to set our hearts on things above. Thus, verses 1 and 2 together would have us set heart and mind on the treasures of heaven rather than the things of earth.

I would sense that my heart is more easily given to the things above than my mind. My heart's desire is to know God intimately, to receive the greatest measure of His love, and to be filled to overflowing with the fullness of Christ in me. This, certainly, is my heart's desire.

My mind also wants this. But my mind gets sidetracked. Worldly concerns and temptations creep into my thinking and I get diverted from my focus on Him. I believe I need to take ownership of this and commit to a better discipline. I also believe that God will help me if I ask, for His heart is to bless me and draw me to Him.

Lord God,

The desire of my heart is to be sold out completely to You. I surrender my heart fully to you. I also submit my mind and my will to you. I confess that I struggle with worldly thoughts even when I don't want to. I ask You to help me.

Lead me, if You will, to a place of full focus on you. Enable me to take every thought captive to be obedient to Christ. Strengthen me in resolve for I know I cannot achieve this in my own strength.

I love You, and that very love moves me to want to be the absolute best I can be for You. Draw me close. Touch me with Your Spirit. Indeed, fill me to overflowing with the presence and power of Your Spirit in me.

May I know You – Father, Son and Spirit – to a degree that I have never known before. And may I share You with as many as come across my path. Receive my love today. I offer it in all humility and sincerity. Lead me through the day and may my heart and my mind be totally focussed on You. I ask these things of You in Jesus' name. Amen.

On the mountain

Set up the tabernacle according to the plan shown you on the mountain.

Exodus 26.30

I have an expectation to get something, to receive insight, from every part of God's Word contained in His Holy Scriptures. But sometimes the word, the insight, is harder to discern than at others times. I have just read two chapters on God's instructions to Moses concerning the construction and fitting out of the tabernacle. They are extremely detailed passages but they do not readily yield wondrous and amazing revelations from God. Not, at least, any that seem to be relevant and vital to my understanding today of the God I embrace and follow.

But insight may be found if we will seek it out. And I believe verse 30 is the key for me. God has called Moses to the mountain. He has removed him from the ordinary in order to give him special instructions and to make a specific impartation to him. On the mountain God shows Moses the plan for the tabernacle. He then gives him details of the plan in the greatest degree of accuracy. Wow! What a revelation!

God has a plan for each one of his children. Sometimes He will call us away from daily chores and responsibilities, and He will declare something of His plan for us. Sometimes what we see will be a mere glimpse, and this might often tease and frustrate us. Sometimes God will unfold for us more of the details of his plan. These might well cause excitement to rise in us. Rarely, however, will God reveal the timing of His plan. This is perhaps to remind us all that it is His plan, and it will come to pass in His perfect time.

Lord God,

I rejoice in the message You have just revealed to me. I confess that the detailed description of the tabernacle and its furnishings did not seem to be telling me much of Your Word for me today. But as I looked, You spoke. Thank You, Lord. Thank You for the love You have for me which speaks to me through all that is written in Your Name.

I thank You for the plan You have for my life. As much as I am able, I commit myself into the fullness of Your plan. I have no idea where I am headed. And I rejoice to say that it doesn't bother me. I trust You, Lord, and I'm almost ready to explode with excitement as I say these words. I will walk with You. I may falter, and I ask You to strengthen and guide me. I may fail, and I ask You now to forgive me, for my heart is for You. I want to live entirely for You. Take me, make me Yours, in Jesus' name I pray. Amen.

Forsaken

And at the ninth hour Jesus cried out in a loud voice, "Eloi, Eloi, lama sabachthani?" – which means, "My God, my God, why have you forsaken me?"

Mark 15.34

Much has been written – in the gospels and beyond – of man's inhumanity to Jesus. The Jewish leaders targeted Him. The mob was swayed to despise and spurn Him, and the Roman authorities were persuaded to give him over to death in a most cruel form – crucifixion, appointed under the Roman system for the common criminal, the lowest of the low! Before handing Him over, the soldiers brutalised Him. On the way to the cross, He was jeered at, ridiculed and spat on by the crowd. All trace of dignity was taken from Him.

Yet the power of the cross is contained in the simple words, *"My God, my God, why have you forsaken me?"*

Man's cruel acts to the Christ, the chosen One, do not affect eternal life. It is God's forsaking – of His own, and only, Son – that brought about eternal life, for all those who would receive Him. When God's perfect Son took upon Himself the sins of all mankind, the spiritual deformity this created in Him was far, far greater than any physical disfigurement or depravity that He bore. The sinless Father turned in horror from the sin-carrying Son, leaving Him utterly alone. And the Son received this rejection. With all the pain of the universe upon Him, He surrendered Himself to the ultimate pain of rejection by His own Father. And in this one single act mankind is redeemed.

Lord Jesus,

Thank You for the release You brought through the extreme pain You suffered on the cross. Even as I write these words, I am being further impacted by the true agony of the crucifixion – not the inhuman treatment You received at the hands of men, but the horror of rejection by the perfect One, Your own heavenly Father.

You paid the price for us all. I thank You. Help me, with further revelation of this amazing act. Help me to spread the word, in Your sweet name I ask. Amen.

Bibliography

Chambers, Oswald. 1927, *My Utmost for His Highest,* Marshall Morgan and Scott Publications Ltd. Marshall Pickering, Basingstoke, UK.

Strong, James. Undated, *The Exhaustive Concordance of the Bible,* Riverside Book and Bible House, Iowa Falls, Iowa, USA.

The Lockman Foundation. 1997, *New American Standard Bible Text Edition,* Foundation Publications, Inc., Anaheim, California, USA.

Unger, Merrill F. And White, William, Jr., Editors, 1985, *Vine's Complete Expository Dictionary of Old and New Testament Words,* Thomas Nelson Publishers, Naxhville, Tennessee, USA

Index of Headings

Index of Scripture